Praise for *Invisible*

"Combining moving personal narratives and social history, this timely book challenges anti-Asian racism and internalization of white norms that contribute to the invisibility of Asian Americans. It uses an intersectional approach to articulate a theology of visibility that decenters whiteness and offers a vision for our collective future. Written in an accessible way, this book can be used in classrooms, churches, and adult forums."
— Kwok Pui Lan, Candler School of Theology, Emory University

"Without Grace Ji-Sun Kim's work, the invisible would not have been made visible and we, especially males, would remain in the dark about the sufferings and travails of Asian women immigrants in the United States. Kim's *Invisible* is an eloquent clarion call to steep American theology in the sufferings and pains and joys and hopes of Asian women. I most strongly recommend this book to all Americans, especially in the current anti-immigration climate."
— Peter C. Phan, Ignacio Ellacuria Chair of Catholic Social Thought, Georgetown University

"*Invisible* opens our eyes to the long history of racism, discrimination, and xenophobia that Asian Americans have faced and are facing. We need a theology of visibility to start embracing, welcoming, and loving one another. I highly recommend this book."
— Susan M. Shaw, professor of women, gender, and sexuality studies, Oregon State University

INVISIBLE

INVISIBLE

THEOLOGY AND THE EXPERIENCE
OF ASIAN AMERICAN WOMEN

GRACE JI-SUN KIM

FORTRESS PRESS
MINNEAPOLIS

INVISIBLE
Theology and the Experience of Asian American Women

Cover image: Shutterstock/LanKS
Cover design: Brad Norr

Print ISBN: 978-1-5064-7092-4
eBook ISBN: 978-1-5064-7094-8

우리 할머니에게 드립니다

Contents

INTRODUCTION

The Invisible Me

Invisibility persists throughout the Asian American story. Occupying a vague social status, the Asian American has long been perceived as a deferential foreigner, an individual with economic significance who exercises their inherent diligence in academic and professional spaces but possesses little social importance. The Asian American remains meek in the dominant American imagination—taking place in the quiet, homogenous, resigned, productive, and advancing enclaves of society. While a sense of rapid growth, competence, and social apathy dominates the present stereotype of Asian Americans, only a century ago, Asian Americans were perceived as illiterate, unappealing, "filthy and disease-ridden,"[1] unassimilable and marginal members of the human race who were denied the right to become naturalized American citizens and were instead segregated to isolated ethnic enclaves.

Despite the various challenges Asian Americans have faced, they are rarely considered worthy of discussing as a community because they do not seem to contend with the same limitations and polarizing concerns that other racial minorities seem to face. As a result,

1

Asian Americans are widely excluded from mainstream discussions of race in this country, erased into obscurity amid an American racial paradigm that shifts obsessively between Black-and-white oppositions. Asian Americans do not fit in on either side and thus remain in an unstable state where they can be designated as good or bad depending on political tempers—becoming emblems of the "model minority" one moment and foreign threats the next.

Even more indiscernible in America's racial landscape are Asian American women. The compounded effects of a patriarchal Asian culture and a white-dominant American culture are formidable, steadily removing these women from America's field of vision. Most Asian American women occupy a more enclosed, hidden sociocultural space than their male counterparts. They are not afforded the same responsibilities or freedoms within their communities, and outside of their communities, they are often forced to challenge the stereotypical image of the Asian American female that predominates: a submissive, sexualized, exotic being. Subsequently, most Asian American women have been denied their agency and have had their distinctive voices stifled behind community walls. Such invisibility, particularly in regard to issues pertaining to gender discrimination and sexual or domestic violence, has continued the legacy of shame that courses through the history of all Asian women. Furthermore, the Asian American church—a place where immigrants have gathered for safe, separate congregation and socialization outside white society—puts women in places of secondary importance, relegating their work to domestic, supportive roles meant to uplift male leaders and organizers. In a place that provides the opportunity for leadership, particularly in a society that permits sparse room for Asian American leaders, these churches deny women the chance for empowerment. The strong patriarchal framework both in the church and in Asian culture perpetuates such ongoing marginalization. The hybrid, liminal spaces that Asian American women occupy turn into barely visible shadows. It is vital that Asian American women resurrect their histories, experiences, and stories from obscurity.

My story is like many who were born in Asia and brought to America: we are immigrant children who psychologically live

within our parents' generational sacrifice—often in a state of repa-
ration for their sufferings—while also harboring our own growing
personal ambitions and desires to explore ourselves outside of familial and cultural expectations. My story is not much different from
women in my mother's generation or those who came before her.
However, unlike them, I have the opportunity to share not just my
own story but the stories of Asian American women in a historical
and contemporary context. In doing so, I hope to provide greater
insight into the Asian American female consciousness so others can
gain a better understanding of our history and interpretation of the
world.

Racism

Since their first major arrival in the United States in the 1850s,
Asian Americans have been degraded by Eurocentric standards of
race and othered in American society. First as indentured workers
in Hawaii and on the mainland, they were hobbled by laws, actions,
and behaviors that legitimized racist attitudes and facilitated social
oppression. This oppression came to the fore through congressio-
nal laws such as the Chinese Exclusion Act, Japanese internment
during World War II, and the denial of voting rights to Asian immigrants. Asian Americans also experienced racism through negative
language and stereotypes and were given labels such as *perpetual
foreigner*, *honorary white*, and *model minority*[2]—all of which minimized the Asian American plight.

Myths created by white mainstream society have followed
Asian Americans for decades, falsely elevating the Asian minority as
the model for other minorities to emulate while suppressing Asian
Americans' real concerns because of their presumed prosperity. The
"model minority" stereotype ignores the reality of Asian American economic life, as they exhibit the greatest economic disparity
among any other racial group in the United States. These labels and
stereotypes become integrated into the consciousness of minorities,
facilitating the harmful internalizations of these false perceptions.
For Asian Americans who are able to consume and perform such stereotypes in dominant spaces, this internalized racism allows for the

continued ignorance of discrimination against them in often sub-
dued, innocuous expressions. These false notions of success and prosperity have hidden the truths of Asian Americans' lived experiences,
rendering them as socially peripheral and culturally insignificant.

Invisibility

Though Asian Americans have been part of American society
since the mid-1850s, they have been consistently made invisible
through marginalization and the troubled understanding that
Asian American issues are not civil rights issues. As distant, minor,
"honorary whites," their experiences of racism are diminished. The
contemporary invisibility of Asian Americans begins at this point
of misunderstanding.

The dominant white culture minimizes Asian Americans
because white people feel no sense of urgency around them. There
have been many instances when either I or someone else shared
experiences of racism and had them immediately downplayed.
Friends, colleagues, and ministers would look at me plainly after
hearing me confess things that had been said to me, telling me,
"That isn't *that* racist," "It could be worse," or "It's not *that* bad for
Asians."

In the Bible, the concept of invisibility is prominent in such
stories as the foreign women in the book of Ezra, the lepers, the
Samaritan woman, and Mary Magdalene. Invisibility as a theological concept can help us understand the dynamics of human interaction, teaching us to be more cognizant of oppressed peoples. It
is important to recognize that as much as invisibility is a societal
issue, it is also a spiritual one—and this is especially important in
discussions surrounding the church.

The Western church has historically masked the concerns of
Asian Americans. This has caused great damage to Asian American
women, who often already exist under oppressive circumstances
within their community. Being part of God's "kin-dom" should
confer agency, voice, and recognition.[3] Asian Americans, and
Asian American women specifically, represent a significant body
of discounted people. The marginalization of Asian Americans

is becoming increasingly important to address as the center of Christianity shifts from Europe to the Global South and the East. Asian and white Eurocentric theologies will continue to influence one another. Therefore, Western theology must decenter, in tandem with globalization, and welcome Asian American voices and doctrines.

Asian American women's voices are necessary. They are essential in the quest to bring all the complexity and richness of Asian philosophy, religion, culture, and heritage to a liberative, reimagined theology. As Asian American women construct a theology of visibility, they uplift the voiceless and empower the invisible, moving beyond experiences of oppression and toward claimed spaces in the kin-dom of God. We seek that union, and we seek that others join in so that the wider society can understand, honor, and dignify Asian American women as full members of the kin-dom of God.

1

MOTHERLAND

War and Comfort Women

When a woman develops in a culture in which discrimination, diminishment, and dismissal are normalized, it often takes a long time for her to confidently express her vocality and visibility. Even as these gifts are being nourished, she can get blindsided by old patterns, behaviors and positionings. And as she gains confidence in her value and self worth, she must also deal with a strange mix of resentments toward others and herself.

In 1995, I was twenty-six years old and beginning my PhD in systematic theology at the University of Toronto. During one of my first courses in the early fall semester, I sat alone in the front of the lecture hall waiting for class to begin. There was a blank yellow notepad in front of me along with three blue pens, lined up, waiting to be used.[1]

As usual, I was early. I was thinking about what I was going to get for lunch that day, wondering whether I had any change at the bottom of my bag for a coffee, and debating whether the new sweater I was wearing was too tight. Behind me, the door opened and closed, and the hurried traffic of a filling classroom thrummed

7

in the increasingly warm, sunlit room. The professor walked in, and as if to signal the beginning of class, a man's voice behind me rang out, "Thank God, another Asian!" Eyes turned toward me. I looked back and saw a small group of young male Asian students, who were clearly friends with one another but mere acquaintances with me, walking through the door. At first, I wondered whether I knew them from somewhere.

Then, feeling increasing attention, I imagined all the people in the room associating me with the male students in their minds, unanimously acknowledging me as the "other Asian" and thus a natural part of their group. Being recognized as a peer—an inherent part of their tribe, a body contained under the shamed title *Asian*—made me resent them deeply at that moment and, even more, made me resent myself.

The Angst of Being the Asian

The seminary classroom experience was not the first time I had been singled out in public for being Asian, female, and an immigrant. I had grown up in what was then the very white community of London, Ontario, which still had a long way to go when it came to embracing minorities. I was accustomed to varying degrees of discrimination, from landlords prohibiting me from entering buildings after simply looking at me, to the quintessential eye pulls and "Ching-chong" chants at elementary school, to myriad comments about how good my English was, to the intense patriarchy of my Korean household. I was no stranger to prejudice and even embraced it as the comfortable heart of commiseration with others like me.

However, as I matured, the unquestionable magnetism I sensed with other Asians also drove me to periodically distance myself from them. Though I had no self-awareness of it at the time, I now recognize that this dissonance originated from an internalized form of the white male gaze. I believe many minorities possess this duplicitous consciousness as a reflexive form of self-protection, among other things. Back then, I feared that if I were to be viewed as another Asian in a group of Asians, I would be minimized to the mere idea of an ethnic tribe—rather than viewed as an individualized, complex person—through the validating eyes of white people; it seemed it was them who had authority over who I was in society and what I represented in the world.

From the Chinese Exclusion Act of 1882 to the recent uptick in hate crimes during the coronavirus pandemic, the history of Asians in America has been one of violence, xenophobia, repression, and assimilation. It has also been, to an extent far less appreciated, one of triumphant innovation and radicalism.

Asian Americans have always had a peculiar relationship with their own identity—one that is rather vague and unsettled. Many have been raised to fulfill the warped promise of the American dream. A vast majority are driven toward this purpose by unbreakable loyalty to their families and communities. As a way of honoring their parents' sacrifices, they have been taught to compete against one another, to work harder than all the rest, and to earn the approval of white people in an attempt to gain success in this country. They have been praised as a "model minority" for their diligence, intellect, and amenability while also being trivialized through the hypersexualization of Asian women and the emasculation of Asian men.

To make matters worse, Asian Americans are often the first to reduce and satirize themselves. I, like so many others, have always been caught in this fight for approval, acceptance, and success, struggling against the contradiction of self-hatred and praise in the confusing trap of Asian American consciousness.

When I was called out as "another Asian" during that early PhD class, I felt a certain anxiety that was long dormant resurge. I was being seen in the room as an Asian, defined solely by my ethnicity while simultaneously being erased as a person with unique visibility and vocality.

While I am remorseful for my resentment toward those students, I must admit that a small part of me still harbors a seed of that feeling. Not against the Asian man who spoke—or my being associated with the group of Asians or even being racially differentiated—but against my being acknowledged purely *because* I was Asian. That is, I was being acknowledged only to be tokenized. Although I am now known as an Asian American theologian or a Korean American theologian (I even regard myself in such a way), I have constantly felt troubled by the idea of being a delegate or face for an entire ethnicity or race. I feel both empowered and confined by the title that has followed me, and I wonder whether there will ever be a time when I will be known as simply a theologian. Then again, I wonder whether there will also be a time when I will not feel so unsettled by it.

The predicament for Asian Americans is that our work cannot be separated from our identity. Asian American women carry the weight of representing their racial identity in their workplaces; they are known only as part of the frail politics of their identity. Racializing their identity is a challenge that is familiar to them, as it is to other ethnic minorities, but it is not something that white people have to perpetually confront. Asian Americans have to deal with this constantly at work. Personally, I experience this as a theologian teaching in a seminary. On the one hand, I feel that I shouldn't constantly have to address my racialized presence in my work, but on the other hand, because there are not many Asian American female voices represented in academia or in literature, I feel that I have an obligation not just to address my racialized identity but to underscore it as a vital part of my work. This plight has always been fraught with tension. In the end, my desire to make certain that an Asian American voice is present has motivated me to claim my racialized identity.

Despite the challenges, my work as a theologian has always provided deeply meaningful rewards. I have the opportunity to reflect and ponder on the notion of who God is. I have the privilege of trying to speak faithfully about God in a way that deepens the theological discourse, broadens the range of conversation partners, and takes seriously the voices that have been absent from the table for the past two thousand years. I have the gift of hope—hope that my theological imagination and creativity can empower other marginalized voices to reimagine a theology that is accepting of all people.

My Invisibility

As time goes on, I look to the younger generations of Asian Americans for a hint of what the future might look like. I see that personal experiences with ethnic identity are more embraced, more unfettered, and if anything, less focal.

I see many young Asian American academics, artists, writers, entrepreneurs, and athletes at the forefront of their respective fields, and I wonder whether they have escaped the trivialization of Asian Americans—if they must escape at all—and, if they have, whether they have done so by evasion, denial, combat, or assimilation.

I wonder whether Asian Americans in my children's generation feel the same conflicted loyalty and resistance toward one another that my generation did. I wonder whether they feel comfortable in a room with other Asian Americans or whether their inner racial angst emerges as it did for me in 1995.

I wonder what it might be like if I were to enter that PhD classroom today, whether I would feel the same unease at being pointed out by another Asian American or whether I might instead find some kind of affectionate coalition.

Perhaps what I really hope is that I wouldn't be pointed out at all—that I might simply be seen in the room and listened to with respect. My invisibility and silence within society, church, and the academy are indicative of this ongoing struggle. To understand why Asian Americans—and in particular, Asian American women—lack visibility and vocality, it is necessary to comprehend the Asian culture that leads to the imperceptibility of Asian women. It is also important to understand immigrant history to see how the hiddenness and silence of Asian Americans are embedded into the very fabric of white dominant society.

The Injustice of Invisibility and Silence

The oppression of Asian American women has long remained behind a veil of silence. Asian American women are still widely viewed as not fully American; instead, they are perceived as foreigners. While a significant part of the problem stems from the social and cultural invisibility of Asian Americans, another crucial element of Asian American women's marginal status is the patriarchal standard that is deeply embedded in Asian culture. Patriarchy has minimized the plight of Asian women and restricted their rights to liberty and justice through ongoing oppression.

The widespread ignorance of this injustice is something many Asian American women have felt. Enforced invisibility was present from my childhood, to my adolescence, and into my adulthood, simultaneously reminding me of what I was to other people while depriving me of my full development and empowerment as an individual. I have discovered what people expect of Asian women through the various stereotypes used to label and control us: there is the geisha type, whose passive submission is accentuated with her eroticization; the dragon lady, whose deceitful dominance derogates the submissive female Asian convention; and finally, the quiet, opinionless, conscientious worker bee. Across all stereotypes, however, Asian women have been most generally regarded as subservient, faceless, invisible objects. These perceptions that once informed the expectations of who I was meant to be now push me to challenge these enduring, unjust misunderstandings.

Asian Americans have been part of American society since the 1500s, but they remain largely invisible through either marginalization or the continuation of the belief that the injustices Asian Americans face are not civil rights issues. The latter may be, in part, attributed to the notion that Asian Americans are viewed by many in the dominant white society as "honorary whites." As such, their experiences of racism tend to be diminished or ignored, while some Asians who speak little English and live steadfastly within their ethnic diaspora are called "unassimilable."

For instance, my mother spoke sparse, broken English. When I was a child, I witnessed countless white adults who were condescending to my mother, dumbing down their words and smiling or laughing when she couldn't understand. Behind those smiles and laughs, I saw their pride and feelings of superiority. The shame I felt during these encounters never went away. I did not have the vocabulary to confront the dominant culture that continued to gaslight me. As time went on, layers of shame, anger, melancholy, and paranoia stifled my psyche, accumulating from all my experiences that were never acknowledged and never truly shared.

There was dissonance between my home life, where I was expected to speak perfect Korean, and my life outside the home, where I had to try to speak perfect English. The negative perceptions I was burdened with due to my poor English led me to repress all my negative emotions tied to language. But reflecting back now, I embrace broken English as one of the great beauties in hearing people speak, as people from all over the world inflect their homes, their histories, into their words. It reminds me of the benefits of being raised bilingual, as you realize how significant yet slippery meaning can be depending on context.

Asian Americans are also largely invisible in the area of political representation, as they are often seen as apolitical. For instance, in the 2020 primary elections, Asians were not even included in the racial breakdowns in polls. They were simply listed as "Other"—if they were listed at all. Despite Asian Americans being regarded as the prosperous model minority, they are left out of essential discussions. Because Asian Americans are so statistically invisible, it feels as though they are not publicly participating and contributing to change in society.

Asian women are often as invisible in their own communities as Asian Americans are in American politics. However, in the Asian American community, the treatment of women whittles down to tradition rather than racial agenda. Within the traditions of Asian collectivist culture, women are widely encouraged to be the alter egos to men—someone to tend to the home and serve the needs of the family through compliance and acquiescence. Women should perform this role with noble femininity not just in their actions but also in their expressions. The notion of Asian women being seen as giving, tender, and quiet is still widely perpetuated, for the traditions in the East still live strong. Thus, Asian women are often relegated to the house. In the Korean language, the common word for wife is *anae*, which can be directly translated to mean "inside." This derivation clearly indicates that wives should be confined to the household—out of sight and out of earshot. Of course, global social norms are changing, but the codes of masculinity and femininity in a collectivist culture seem to be unyielding for most of society.

Breaking Out of Bearing Pain in Silence

My first home, my first family, my first and only infinite universe is Korea. I spent the first years of my life in Korea not knowing that there were any other places. The land I occupied was the only land that existed. The people I saw were the only people who I thought existed. There were no other countries, no other bodies, and no other points of difference indicating to me, in some remarkable or intelligible way, that I possessed any qualities that marked me as an individual.

Reflecting on this period of blank beauty, unconsciousness, and utter ambivalence, I look back at my early childhood in Korea with a strange feeling. Perhaps it is simply because it has come to represent the mythos of a beginning when everything was good, when my identity was intact and, arguably, could have stayed so. But perhaps it is also because, like all good things, it came to an end; passed time revealed the flaws of my idealized childhood. Like so many things about my past, this feeling of loss is predicated on the oscillating core of the Asian American immigrant experience—a shared history of yearning and alienation, suppression and innovation. Because of my experiences, I am torn about my motherland. Korea symbolizes an end of a beginning, where so many good memories became inflected with the chaos of the after, where my Korean core became inflected with my growing American self.

The centerpiece for what came to define my "Asian American identity" was a romantic vision I invented after I moved. That move, my family's immigration to Canada in the mid-1970s, separated my life into a clear before and after. Korea was *before*.

I was born in 1969 in Seoul, Korea, and lived there until I immigrated to Canada at the age of five. Though Korea was under intense economic strains from increasing income disparity between the industrial and agricultural sectors, my family had no anxiety about money. Nearly every day, my mother took my sister and me out to the shopping streets where we would languidly stroll about. While everyone else seemed to be working hard, opening their vendor stalls at 4:00 or 5:00 a.m. to prepare cuts of meat or make endless varieties of fresh and aged kimchi, my mother took her time in the mornings, preparing a simple breakfast and making sure both her daughters had bathed and brushed their hair into perfect little black bobs. Then, checking us over before we went into town, she'd take us into narrow streets where we would snack on sweet buttered corn and hot roasted chestnuts while eyeing shiny new things.

Often, my mother would take my sister and me window-shopping, and we would envision ourselves as grown women wearing what the shop display mannequins had on. One day, my sister and I admired our reflections over *hanboks*, traditional Korean dresses. Our mother took notice and suggested that we take a quick look. Inside the store, we gazed up at fluffy silk walls filled with vivid red, green, fuchsia, and yellow dresses. My mother quickly picked out red and fuchsia *hanboks* for my sister and me and carried them out in titanic shopping bags. We were beaming. Then on the street, a dirty hand, marred with infected lesions, reached out. When I looked down, I saw a heavily disfigured, legless old man slumped on the ground. Terrified, I began to cry. My mother swept me up without a glance at the man and swiftly walked away. I later asked my mom what was wrong with him, but she didn't spare me any explanation. She simply said, "Don't worry about things like that." But I did, as I came across more and more men like that on the street. Physically plagued with the misfortune of the Korean War, disfigured, drastically scarred and missing their limbs, these men had nowhere to go to and no one to take care of them. Unable to work and provide for themselves, they resorted to begging. This was a time when Korea was trying to cope and recover from the terrorizing effects of the war, which my parents had escaped unscathed—or so I initially believed. The aftermath of the Korean War was also a period of mass orphanhood, mostly girls, as an entire society of people who lost everything simply had no means to raise their children. For the country, the homeless veterans represented the tragic economic loss of the war, but the surge of international Korean adoptions were helpful to Korean society.

While my mother was able to gain some stability soon after the war, getting married and having a family, she was already well acquainted with loss. She was a child of the war. As my mother had seven brothers and sisters, food was a household deity, and after battling to acquire any amount of food she could get her hands on, she had to be diplomatic about sharing with her family. On days when she could not find enough to eat, she gave what she could to her younger siblings and went hungry. In her rare, brief storytelling—always told with sober restraint and reluctance—she told me fragments of her past much later in her life. She broke out of her silence, but only in a very restricted way.

When she was in her early fifties, she had to pass painful kidney stones at the hospital. It was unbearable to watch, and she cried out in so much pain, divulging that she would take childbirth over this. After a few hours of intense pain, they were finally passed, and the doctors put the stones in a little orange prescription bottle. She peered at them with wonder, and then I saw the melancholy seep in. For several days and weeks afterward, I heard them rattling in her pocket. Confused by the constant clatter in her walk, I asked her, "Umma, why do you keep carrying those things around?"

She paused and stuck her hand in her pocket, holding the bottle in her hand. Then, sitting down, she told me they were the sediments of the war—the losses and sorrow that had built up inside of her over all these years had turned to stone. I listened as she told me of how she had to sneak onto nearby farms and sift through the cow manure, picking out corn and grains that were not entirely digested. Then she would do the best she could to clean them and bring them home to share with her brothers and sisters. She looked at me, looked back at the stones, and told me that there was a lot she had to do to save her family, things she could never take back. When I asked her what she meant, she stood up and walked away, letting out a sigh rather than an explanation.

Her stories, while harrowing, are not unique. They are the stories of countless other young women who endured this time, who only knew how to do one thing: survive. She acted in order to live, and she lived in order to ensure that her family survived. Many years later, she didn't want to dwell on the past, or perhaps it was just too painful to talk about.

The torment of the war lived on with the Koreans who survived it. This pain persisted and was passed on in the simplified term *han*, a Korean expression that represents the wider Korean experience of unjust suffering. Condensing the vast and complicated memories of sorrow into a simple word avoids further explanation of the pain.

I often hear *han* described as "the Asian way"—to suppress our deepest feelings inside and then build an impenetrable wall around them. Throughout my life, I have constantly had to reconcile that my parents had entire lives separate from the ones they shared with me, lives that reflect the recurring characters in the Asian American community's history: the sacrificial parents, the silent and passive mother, the overbearing tiger mom, the dominating patriarch. Every generation of Asian Americans feels as though it discovers these stereotypes for the first time. In this way, we are our own mystery. My mother has kept so many stories from me, and her evasive narrative voice echoes that of many other Asian women from her era, which have been kept buried and fossilized, waiting for someone to discover it. It keeps me questioning our understanding of our predecessors, and in turn, it keeps me questioning what we really know about ourselves. Patient and respectful curiosity can break through the silencing impact of pain. Invisibility and silence deprive us of so much. By the end of the conversations I had with my mother, I had only an inkling of all that had yet to be said.

The Pain of Patriarchy

On my mother's side of the family, I have four uncles and three aunts, and on my father's side, I have two uncles and three aunts, and all these aunts and uncles went on to have multiple children—so suffice it to say, I have a big extended family. I have what seems like a hundred cousins. Like any large family gathering, ours are chaotic. But when I was a child, since I didn't have many friends at pre-school, I was excited to be amid the chaos because I had enough "friends" there to last me a lifetime.

As I navigated my way through the different social groups within the family, I discovered the infallible gaze of one man, the black sheep, the scary one: "Tiger Uncle." He was my mother's brother, but he had the honor of having his own nickname.

Tiger Uncle was the odd man out, the one who had eyes that commanded the room. For us kids, these eyes told us to *behave*. His powerful stare stopped us in our tracks, and he became the ghoulish character of our world—the one we would actively avoid and even more actively discuss. My cousins and I always hid from him and would play in out-of-the-way places, but inevitably, when one of us got into trouble, he sprung out of nowhere with his punishing eyes, holding a long wooden spoon. I was so scared, I would run straight under my mother's skirt and hide until he left. I think he took great joy in this.

Despite the fact he had his own family, he was always telling my mother what to do, how to spend her money, and how to discipline her children. She obeyed him naturally without question. As a child, this Tiger Uncle came to embody Asian patriarchy. His expectation of strict female obedience and being served hand and foot was normative Asian male behavior. My uncle couldn't even get his own glass of water to drink; instead, a woman in the house had to bring it to him. This was a common scenario in a Korean household, and it was something I was very much accustomed to, as my own father behaved in the same way. Based on Confucian ideals, Asian patriarchal culture stipulates that a man is the leading provider of the family; thus, he is meant to be served by his family/wife domestically, emotionally, and physically. The women living in the house are tasked with doing everything they can to maintain the family and household in peace, often compensating their own agency for the needs of the husband. My Tiger Uncle represented how the traditional Korean household functioned. He was the archetypal Asian male who held emotional and financial authority over women.

Models of Invisible and Silent Female Pain

My paternal grandmother was an exception of her time. A forceful businesswoman and independent mother, she possessed a stoic presence that could never be rendered invisible. Unlike the conventional Korean women of her time, she worked outside of the home, supervising payrolls and employees, managing an enterprise that began with nothing but a desperate single mother without work but with mouths to feed.

When I think of my grandmother, I am reminded of her physiognomy, her natural expression. Her face was carved from hardship, from the years of hard labor, war, abuse, stress, and loss that left it stern and worried. I don't recall ever seeing her smile or laugh, frown or panic; she had become stuck in a face that had to look serious to be taken seriously. Her seriousness puzzled me, and I remember watching her as a child and wondering if she would ever crack a smile.

During the periods we stayed with her in Korea, I remember peeking into her bedroom every night and watching her sit on the floor motionless, staring at the wall. I would wait to see her move, but there wasn't a stir in the room. She simply sat there for hours, lost in thought.

I can remember that every morning, still under a sleepy trance, she would instinctively walk herself to her black dresser. There was a vanity mirror—large enough to reflect the lower half of her body when standing—fixed over a wide middle drawer that held the distant prizes of womanhood: colorful jewelry, hairpins, lipstick, bottled creams, and perfume that I would spray on the inside of my sleeve in secret.

On either side of the mirror were smaller drawers that neatly housed books, papers, and documents. It was an ornate, indulgent piece of furniture in an otherwise plain room; it had a glossy lacquered black surface that beamed with an elaborate pearl inlay of swirling, symmetrical, intricate flowers, cranes and butterflies. I would observe her sitting on the floor in front of the dresser and taking out a jewelry box made of seashells. This was my personal favorite, and I remember watching her open it to reveal another small mirror that swung open and propped up. Though she wore no makeup, she did her hair every morning in this little mirror, spinning the thin white strands in her fingers and giving them a good brush. Then she parted her hair clean down the middle, twisted it into a single spiral, and tied it into a bun at the nape of her neck. Her hair, like her face, never moved and remained in a tight coil to relieve her of any possibility that it would loosen during the day.

My grandmother had three children with her husband before he passed away and left her a widow. Then, with another man who already had a wife, she had another three. This man had six daughters with his wife before he decided to have a relationship with my grandmother, supposedly because his wife was not able to bear him any sons. In my grandmother's time, it was very common for men to have concubines or other women to help bear a son if their first chosen partner could not. My grandmother was a clear part of this practice, something that manifested from a Confucian-led Korea that saw a woman's life purpose as bearing sons for men. Her first child with this man was his first and only son, my father.

My grandfather was ecstatic about this news, as he finally had his first successor after having a disappointing six daughters. The hope for a son still stands in Korean culture, though it is less apparent today. But especially then, a woman expecting a child always had a family in high anticipation of a son. After having my father, my grandmother had two more daughters with the same man. They were never married; he simply went around to my grandmother's house for his own sexual needs.

Though I never knew him well, I knew him as a tall, broad, handsome man who smoked. He came over often to my grandmother's house—so much that I actually thought that they were living together or married. I had no idea that he had a wife and a large family elsewhere until I was an adult. He passed away when I was about seven years old, so I don't have that many memories of him, though what my father shared about him was not the least bit flattering.

My father told me of how he would frequently see his father storm into the house unannounced, swinging open the door abruptly and ripping my grandmother away from whatever she was doing. He would drag her out by her hair, frustrated about something out of her control, and beat her without saying more than a few words. He knocked her over to the floor as she covered her face with her hands. Then he slammed, hit, and kicked her until he tired himself out. My father was always small and weak, and he admitted to me that he was so terrified by his father that he would run and hide in the wardrobe, where he had to listen in fear to the sounds of his mother "learning a lesson."

The abuse was ongoing and, unsurprisingly, private. After my grandfather left to go home to his wife and family, my grandmother picked herself up, saying nothing, and went on. She had no time to confront her suffering and certainly no time to let herself be affected by it. She would wake up the next morning while it was still dark out, never showing a flicker of vulnerability. She went on like this for years, and I imagine she put all her frustration and suffering into her work. Eventually, she became a wealthy woman all on her own, and her ability to feed and raise her family was completely contradictory to what an unmarried woman should be able to achieve at the time, especially considering her ongoing abuse.

In Asian culture, it is very difficult to speak up against abuse. My grandmother and women like her endured in silence. Their society did not value women's bodies, emotional health, or psychological needs. Abuse is one of the most appalling accepted behaviors that has remained in Korean culture across generations. It is understood that women are abused at the hands of their husbands and fathers, and it is understood that they will just suffer through it, work through it, and succeed through it. In a patriarchal culture, physical and sexual abuse are seen as ways for men to discipline women, who have been painted as obedient, subservient, and enduring of suffering. Women endure pain silently and privately, as being vocal is a sure way of bringing shame onto themselves and thereby their whole family.

This carries on the cyclical nature of abuse, as the abused women go on to allow their children to suffer violence only to become violent themselves as they mature into adulthood. These children learn by example, bringing what they see as "normal" behavior into the next generation. The abused hide the nature of the violence done unto them, justifying it through any means, harboring it with great shame.

The pattern repeated itself in my family. My father grew up alongside extreme, silent violence, and the actions he once witnessed became adopted and normalized in my household. Abuse, shame, and ultimately, the frustrating and resounding quietness of my mother were prominent. My mother was yet another silent sufferer.

If there was one thing that people knew about my mother, and there was not much that people knew, it was that she was a woman of few words. She rarely spoke. She had a silence about her that at times deeply troubled me; at other times, it infuriated me. I could not understand how she could not react in any other way to my father's anger and abuse than through silence. It saddened me as I saw her struggle to form any relationships outside her turbulent family life; above all, it mystified me.

Sometimes a person can be by your side your whole life and still remain a stranger. My mother was one such person. I feel that there is still so much I never knew about her, so many things about a history adamantly kept a secret, and so many sides to a persona that whispered on the surface.

War and Poverty

Like my father, my mother's behavior directly reflected her experience with her family. Despite the afflictions of the war and the desperate poverty that her family encountered, my mother always said that her home was calm and genial. She was the fifth child in a family that eventually grew to have eight children: an equal four daughters and four sons. When I asked her if her parents fought like her and my dad when she was a girl, she solemnly replied that she had never seen her parents fight. She had never heard so much as a raised voice, and from my limited experience with my maternal grandparents, neither had I. Their home was exceptionally quiet. Her parents, like her, were people of very few words.

My maternal grandmother stood at a full-bodied five foot two and always maintained her serenity. My mother inherited my grandmother's traits: the cheerful look, soft facial features, and a comfortable pair of reading glasses perched at the tip of her nose. When she spoke, my maternal grandmother let the words flow out with ease—totally contrary to my paternal grandmother, who thought cautiously about everything she said and barely let anything slip out of her pressed lips. She was a carefree woman, and I remember her being fun despite all the difficulties she could have easily let drive her into cynicism or even despair.

My grandmother had a large scar on her left thigh. It looked like a huge, grotesque dimple with scarred stitches all around it. I had always wondered where she got it from, and when I was about nine years old, I finally found the courage to ask. During the Korean War, as she was fleeing Seoul with her seven young children, she stepped on a land mine. When it exploded, the shrapnel went right through her thigh, nearly destroying her leg but saving her child from getting hit instead. She hid that scar, but she was not ashamed of it.

Like my paternal grandmother, my maternal grandmother also had a jewelry box, but hers was made not of beautiful pearlescent seashell but of dark unfinished wood. It had no vanity mirror encased or lining inside, nor was there any jewelry or valued memorabilia. But instead, there was candy. Grandma loved candy. As a young girl, whenever I went to visit her, the wooden box loomed in my mind. I would beg for a single piece, and she would always offer some, tenderly so. I think she liked the idea of her granddaughter chasing her around and asking for something she knew she was able to give.

From my limited memories of my mother's father, I don't recall him ever uttering a single word. He was tall, with a long, serene face and a slight physique. According to my mother, he was the kindest person she had ever known. She told me how thoughtful he was, especially with her mother. By the time I knew him, he was weak and often sick. I remember that while Grandma always entertained and played with my sister and me, he sat or laid down on the floor mat quietly in his room, suffering from an unknown illness.

My mother loved her father, and it was a great shock to her after girlhood to discover that not all men were as good-natured. For as long as I can remember, my mother had no significant family memorabilia, but the one thing she carried with her was a tiny black-and-white photo of her father, less than three inches tall and two inches wide. He was in his early thirties, wearing an elegant black suit, looking as strong and beautiful as a storybook hero. Like my mother, he had cropped, thick, wavy hair; full, straight brows; and sensitive eyes. The photo was pressed flat within a Bible, where it periodically slipped out, reminding her that he was still with her. Because it was not in an album or frame, it was unprotected, which confused me. It seemed like a careless way to keep one of the few photos of him. But in this way, my mother was able to periodically hold the picture in her palm, feeling the aged cardstock between her fingers.

My mother was very secretive about her family and went out of her way to keep parts of her upbringing hidden. She had been deeply ashamed of being raised in poverty, in part because her husband's family was wealthy. This disparity enhanced the power dynamics already extant between a husband and wife. As a result, my mother was wary to tell me anything about her family. She didn't want her children to think that her family was poor, uneducated, and from a low social class.

Like American society, Korean society deeply reveres wealth and idolizes upward mobility and success; however, Korean society is not so subtle in its patronization of the poor. My mother's family resided in Seoul, in a tiny house with a small dirt courtyard, *madang*, where they would wash themselves and their clothes and hang their laundry to dry. At the entrance was a dark metal gate that bore a frame with broken glass laid overtop to deter anyone from intruding, which was common in their area. The front of the home was surrounded by six-foot gray stone walls upheld with clay so that strangers and onlookers would not be able to see in. The house was composed of three main rooms separated by thin paper walls. The living room was in the center of the home, flanked by two small bedrooms that sat across from each other.

Since my mother's family was large, they slept throughout the three rooms, using them simultaneously as their bedroom, living space, dining space, and work space. They had an outhouse out front, which was dark, rank, and absolutely terrifying. Even more terrifying was their kitchen. Upon entrance, the bedroom on the right was adjacent to a set of stairs—four meager wooden steps—that led down to an insulated windowless room. This cellar was the kitchen, which had a frigid cement floor, a large wood stove, and peculiar dried and dead oddities hanging from the ceiling. It smelled like many things, but most of all, it smelled like the quintessential Korean aroma of fermenting pickled cabbage, kimchi. I was much too afraid to enter what I thought was a dungeon, so I peeked at it from the stairs as I watched my grandmother bravely enter to cook a family feast.

Unlike my mother's very mild, health-conscious cooking, my grandmother cooked with tons of salt. When she visited Canada later in life, I remember once watching her prepare *kim*, a dry-roasted and seasoned seaweed, which she would douse with salt. My mother gasped theatrically and asked her why she was putting in so much salt, and my grandmother responded with a simple answer: they would only need a tiny tear to eat with their rice. People typically eat *kim* in organized cut sheets, blanketed over spoons of rice, but even decades after the war, my grandmother still always rationed everything. It was a constant battle to survive in her family, one that was well concealed in salt and extra spoons of sugar. My mother had the same tendency and rationed small, illogical things like toilet paper and toothpaste, habitually measuring everything in case it were to run out suddenly. My mother and grandmother lived with scarcity mentalities. Yet living in poverty was not the only source of limitation or hardship for them; patriarchy and gender roles not only restricted their behavior but oppressed them physically and psychologically.

The Rigid Conventions of Confucian Patriarchy

Korean patriarchy arose most dominantly from the teachings of Confucianism, which was adopted as the official Korean religion during the Yi dynasty (1392–1910 CE) and led to restraints on women's social freedoms. Confucianism's moral code for women is strict and oppressive, and it profoundly shaped the collective Korean consciousness and cultural development of the country.[2]

To understand Korean culture, it is important to comprehend how Confucianism views society in terms of personal and ethical relationships. The five key relationships are ruler-subject, father-son, husband-wife, elder brother–younger brother, and friend-friend. Three of these are familial relationships, but all are conceived in terms of the family model. In general, Confucian society regards itself as a large family, and each member has mutual and reciprocal responsibilities based on a hierarchy. Each relationship type emphasizes an authority figure as higher in the hierarchy—the ruler, the father, the husband, and the elder brother. The only horizontal relationship, or relationship of equals, is between friends (49, 50). The family and a sense of community are essential elements of

Confucian society. By stressing the essential values of filial piety, humanness, and ritual, Confucianism was fixed on maintaining the status quo. It focused on the vertical order of relationships based on age, sex, and social status (48).

Deriving in large measure from the Confucian tradition, Korean women's history is dominated by patriarchal religion, thought, and culture. Confucianism played a major role in determining women's lives: how they are to behave, who they are to obey, and what they are to give their lives to (42). The Confucian-based society defined itself through rigid conventions, and the roles of men and women were fixed into binaries with little room for deviation on either side.

Confucianism limited female education to "feminine" virtues and domestic skills; women had to remain in the home, maintain the household, bear children, raise and uphold a family, cook, clean, and support their husbands. Despite their lifelong work and contribution, women are not considered equal to men. In the Confucian ideal, women are passive, obedient, chaste, and subordinate to men. Within the home, men retain all the significant rights and privileges, and the institutional suppression of women extends outside of the home as well. To attain virtue, women must lead lives of complete self-sacrifice, neglecting their own wishes and desires for the sake of the family.[3] These women live not for themselves but for their children and male relatives. Thus, a woman's identity and purpose are not separated from the institutional family.

Ancestor worship, the major ritual of Confucianism, portrays the male as both dominant and supreme. This practice reunites the ancestors with the living family members and thereby strengthens the identity of the family's lineage. The oldest man in the family, the first son, is the ritual priest, and all men participate in the ceremony. Women participate only as men's assistants, and they manage all the necessary preparations, such as cooking the food and setting up the ritual table, but are not actually part of the ceremony. The ritual, then, concretely illustrates the distinct (and opposite) roles assigned to men and women.

Under Confucianism, marriage is a union of two family lines even more than the union of two individual people. In traditional Korean society, young people did not choose their partners, as only parents could arrange a marriage.[4] At marriage, a bride passed out of her natal family and joined the family of her husband. Her first obligation was to honor her husband's parents and ancestors by providing a male heir to continue the line.[5] The more sons a woman produced, the more security the family had in transmitting its name through several generations.[6] This necessity for having sons also offered an excuse for the husband to take on second wives in case the principal wife was childless or had only daughters. The practice of concubinage reduced women to sex objects for men to manipulate, enjoy, and use to gain familial power. Furthermore, this practice was also a constant threat to the first wife, as it brought insecurity and jealousy into the relationship.[7] At best, a woman could hope to get married, become a housewife, perform ancestral sacrifice, give birth to a son, and serve her husband's parents. At worst, she could be forced to serve as a concubine for a sonless man.[8] Thus, the more Confucian Korean society became, the more subordinate, oppressed, and invisible women became to the wider society.

In traditional Korea, unlike men, women were not allowed to exist in public places. Hence, one of the terms for wife is *anae* (inside person). If a woman wanted to participate in social activities, she had to get permission from either her husband or the head of the family.[9] Traditional homes had a *madang* (small outdoor courtyard); the women would stay inside the gates of the home, separated from society, existing primarily in seclusion from the outside world that diminished their rights and social presence. Women were told to stay inside—out of sight and out of the way of men.

Men and women were further segregated within the home. Houses were divided into male and female sections, and it was considered improper for men to enter into the women's section and vice versa unless the master of the house gave his permission.[10] Women were confined to the women's quarters, which were usually the kitchen and the sleeping quarters.

Major Confucian dictums dehumanized women during Korea's Yi dynasty (1392–1910 CE). Women were indoctrinated with the ideology that they were to live in service of men; parents arranged their daughters' marriages; the wife belonged to her husband's family after marriage, seldom able to visit her parents; a wife was regarded only by her husband's or son's name; a woman could not carry on a family line; and daughters could not legally inherit property from their parents.[11] Many of these Confucian teachings and beliefs persist today. Confucian understanding still governs much of women's behaviors, roles, and expectations in Asian societies, enforcing the idea that women are not forced to but should *want* to abide by Confucian standards. This harmful ideology prevails in contemporary America among Asian Americans, who are caught in the restrictive gender roles of their native country and community. These women are challenged with claiming their own power and visibility.

"No Name Woman"

Throughout much of Asian history, women have been written out of history and ignored. In Korean history, many women's names simply were not recorded, and their stories were never passed down to their descendants. Maxine Hong Kingston's book *The Woman Warrior: Memoirs of a Girlhood among Ghosts*, which blends Chinese folktales with her biography, powerfully describes this process.[12] In a chapter entitled "No Name Woman," Kingston illustrates how quickly a woman's existence can be eliminated from memory, understanding, and consciousness. This story embodies the prevalence of women's invisibility throughout much of Korean history.

In the book, Kingston shares the story of her aunt, who died by suicide after giving birth to a girl. The baby girl was conceived with a man other than her husband, who was away at Gold Mountain. This aunt, referred to as the "no name woman," like all other "no name women," existed on the margins of a patriarchal Asian culture that maintained "it was better to raise geese than girls." Women were not valued, and therefore if a woman brought shame to the family, it was better to erase her from family records rather than have her continue to bring shame.

Even in death, this unnamed aunt is punished by being deliberately forgotten and disconnected from the living. She becomes a ghost who is wandering and hungry, thus begging or stealing food from other ghosts who have living kin to give them gifts of food and money. In Asian culture, paying respect to the dead is of great importance. Just as westerners bring flowers to the grave, Asians bring food and drinks to "feed" their relatives. Setting up a table and eating the food is also part of ancestor worship. However, this "no name woman" is undignified, disrespected, and left "homeless" in death. She is a forever-wandering ghost in the afterlife with no one remembering her or feeding her.

This "no name woman" is expunged from the family record, her name erased "as if she had never been born." Much like the countless other women who have been forgotten after death, the "no name woman's" illegitimate child, who died with her, could not have been included within their circle of kin. This is because the child presented a severe challenge to male dominance, having been conceived out of either rape or defiance of "female chastity."[13] This story is a reminder of a recurring event that happens within a patriarchal society: women's actions are crudely interpreted by men who determine the damning consequences. "No Name Woman" is a stark reminder that there are other women made invisible by an oppressive, patriarchal culture.

During Korea's Yi dynasty, women had no names of their own and were identified by their relationship to men (e.g., so-and-so's daughter, so-and-so's wife, and so-and-so's mother). When she married, a woman's family name was entered into her husband's family registry, and her name was removed from her family registry, where only the name of her husband was recorded (55). This omission served to bolster a system of male dominance and privilege.[14] Some remnants of this naming practice still exist, as many Asian women's names are not used after they are married. These women are only referred to by their marital status. Asian American women both inherit and confront this sociocultural history that primarily views them as child-bearers who will continue their husband's family line. Many women who wanted to be free from this burden sought to leave Asia and go to America, where they believed they would have a better life. However, as women left their native countries, they encountered more barriers and burdens.

Invisible and Silenced from Generation to Generation

I share some of the women in my family to provide a window into the lives of Asian women who endured patriarchy, marginalization, silence, and invisibility within their own culture. These structures of patriarchy kept women indoors and silenced them within the public sphere. However, in private, women were being exploited in more insidious ways—not just as bodies to bear sons but as bodies to be used and exploited for the gratification of men's sexual desires. This happened during World War II, when Korean women were taken by the Japanese government to be abused as sexual slaves.

Comfort Women Shamed into Invisibility and Silence

While there are countless examples of the "invisible" Asian women in history, perhaps there is no more resonant of an example of the extremes of invisibility than the "comfort women" of World War II. During the war, the Japanese military systematically kidnapped Korean girls and women to work as sexual slaves for their soldiers and to relieve the men of any anger, trauma, or anguish they experienced in battle. These young women were placed in small quarters and raped by soldiers anywhere from fifty to seventy times a day. The majority of them did not survive, dying either through illness, transmitted disease, suicide, or murder by Japanese officials. The majority of those who did survive never shared their stories due to the shame they harbored. Some took their own lives shortly after returning home, unable to live through the pain of the past; others never got married or had children, being physically unable to bear children from health conditions or believing that their bodies were ruined from sexual slavery. The few who shared their experiences of being comfort women did so at the end of their lives. An even smaller number sought justice. Among them was Kim Bok-dong.[15]

At twenty-one years old, Kim Bok-dong returned to her hometown of Yangsan, South Gyeongsang, South Korea, after an eight-year absence. She was just a girl entering her teens when she had been forced to leave, but despite the fear she had about her departure, she also had hope that she would be able to sustain her family through the promise of a new job. When she returned eight years later, she no longer was the girl who imparted such hope, as her trust in humanity—male humanity—had been shattered. The betrayal she experienced had ravaged her spirit and destroyed her body.

Kim was born in the southeastern region of Korea in March 1926, the fourth of six daughters. In her early youth, her family had been fortunate financially, but later on in her childhood, her golden circumstances fell apart. Her family fell deep into poverty. This struggle was heightened further by the beginnings of World War II and the death of her father when she was only eight years old. To escape poverty, her three older sisters got married one after the other, while Kim remained at home with her mother and two younger sisters.

Under Japanese rule, she saw young Korean boys at school conscripted to fight in World War II as student soldiers, while young women were also forcibly recruited for purposes that seemed equally justifiable.[16] When she was fourteen years old, Japanese authorities knocked on her door to tell her mother that Kim had to be sent off for work. They claimed she would be working in a military clothing factory that was short-staffed and in need of young working women. They promised she would return after three years when she was of legal age to marry. If Kim's family failed to comply, they would be categorized as traitors and lose everything in exile from Korea. Before they took her daughter away, they demanded that Kim's mother sign a document—even though she could not read—that she conceded to in fear and out of the belief that their claims were true. Kim figured that through this option, her family would survive through her support, and she also felt confident in her own survival, as she would be working in a factory rather than becoming a laborer of war.

This was just a single act of coercion in the mass kidnapping and collection of young women, primarily from Korea and China. However, other Japanese-occupied territories were also subject to this recruitment, including Guangdong, Hong Kong, Singapore, Indonesia, and Malaysia. Parents of adolescent girls, mostly aged fourteen to nineteen years old—but including some as young as eleven years old—were promised that their daughters would occupy jobs in nursing or clothing production.[17]

The Japanese Imperial Army had a far more sinister goal in mind: providing comfort stations for their soldiers. In order to prevent the perceived tainting of the Japanese image through previous atrocities—such as the Rape of Nanjing, where Japanese Imperial troops murdered and raped Chinese residents of Nanjing and were later condemned—the Japanese government devised these brothels as legally "consensual" comfort stations. Officials had Kim's mother sign a document because the Japanese government wanted to provide written evidence that these women were involved through their own consent. Comfort stations were planned to prevent hostility among native residents in occupied territories. In other words, the Japanese Imperial Army feared that the seething resentment of their soldiers would result in riot and revolt, so they provided comfort women for their men. In the patriarchal sexual ideologies of East Asian Confucian culture, these comfort women would serve to fortify the soldiers' spirits and provide a cathartic vent for all the frustrations military life created for them.[18] The term *military comfort women*, which is translated literally from the Japanese *Jugun Ianfu* (慰安婦), is an euphemism for forced prostitution—in this case, the systematic and collective rape of women as governed and enforced by the Japanese Imperial Army. The term *comfort women* was meant to disguise the inhumane reality of this work.

Upon her mother's signed consent, Kim Bok-dong was taken to a port in Busan, where she traveled on a night ferry and arrived in Shimonoseki, Japan, in the morning. There were around thirty young women held there, all older than the mere fourteen-year-old Kim. After a few days, they were sent off to Taiwan and then to their final destination in the Chinese province of Guangdong. When she arrived at what she believed was a factory, high-ranking military officers asked her how old she was. They briefly debated about her being too young but ultimately decided she was of acceptable age, and told her to go inside the building, where she was greeted by an army medic team. They briefly examined her body for reasons she was unsure of and sent her off to a dorm that would become her primary residence. From the outside, you could see plainly into the rows of many of these rooms, all the same as the one she was confined to.

The first night, she was dragged into another similar room and beaten by an officer to get her into a submissive, more compliant state. There, as she laid on a hard white bed, a Japanese man entered the room and raped her. She was just entering puberty then, and the pain of the rape left her badly injured and soaked the bed with blood that seeped from between her legs. White sheets, now red, clung to her skin.

She was sent back up to her dorm, where she found two other girls crying because they had endured the same devastating experience. It was then that they all realized the horrific reality of this promised work. They asked one another how they could possibly continue to live like this and ultimately came to a conclusion: that they would be better off dead.[19]

Trying to find methods of suicide, Kim remembered hearing once that people could die from drinking too much alcohol, so she used all the money her mother had given her for food before her departure and asked a cleaning lady who worked in the building if she could buy her something strong enough to knock her out for good. Stunningly, the woman went out and came back with a large bottle of Kaoliang liquor (40–60 percent alcohol), which was split and finished among the two other girls, who fell unconscious soon after. Later, after going missing from their shift, they were found by officials and revived after their stomachs were pumped.

Kim had to endure being raped by twenty-five to forty-five men every day—with some women suffering an unfathomable sixty to eighty rapes a day—for years as the comfort station moved throughout numerous Japanese-occupied territories in Asia. Kim recounted that during this period, she—like the majority of other comfort women—did not speak out, fight back, or resist, as doing so resulted in ruthless beatings, torture, and death. Often, to make an example of a disobedient woman, men at the station would abuse and mutilate her before killing her in front of the other women. While the Japanese government long denied these murders, claiming that they took many measures to ensure the women's survival in camp, the psychological ramifications of authority became a murderous power, and the institution itself had a deeply ingrained notion of these women's disposability. This notion validated the murder of the disobedient, the diseased, and the pregnant so as not to burden the army's men or their military capacities.[20]

Kim's primary hours of work were from 8:00 a.m. to 5:00 p.m. on Sundays and from 12:00 p.m. to around 6:00 p.m. during the other days of the week. Men lined up in long lines outside the women's rooms, eager to be "comforted," often becoming belligerent when the wait was too long. The military men who visited the comfort stations were estimated to have visited once, twice, or three times a month. At the end of these long working days, Kim found herself unable to stand up or walk normally.[21]

Comfort women were divided by their presumed race, class, and nationality, and only men of a certain rank were allowed to visit them according to this hierarchy. Women from Japan, Korea, China, Malaysia, and the Philippines were relegated to lower-class soldiers, whereas European women, primarily Dutch women, were assigned to higher-ranking officials. Often referred to in army and navy documents as "units of war supplies" and, as one Japanese army doctor who was employed at a comfort station put it, "female ammunition," it is revealed that not only were these women exploited as sexual slaves; they were also forced to donate their bodies and blood for wounded soldiers.[22] In 1990, a Dutch victim, Jan Ruff-O'Herne, testified at the US House of Representatives committee that even the Japanese doctor who visited the station raped her each time she was examined for venereal disease.[23] The culture of sexual enslavement had no bounds within the brothels. Though the women were medically treated to uphold high rates of sterility, as the war continued and medical supplies dwindled, some, unbelievably, were billed for treatment, while most were left to die alone when ill.

According to a report issued by Allied forces in 1944, the house master, or commander, of the comfort station received 50–60 percent of the women's gross earnings, which were also determined by how much debt they had incurred from their signed contracts.[24] Many families were misled to believe that their daughters would work in hospitals or factories overseas and signed the contract with an advance of a few hundred yen. This advance was considered debt that the girls had to pay off from their earnings as comfort women.

Girls who were kidnapped by Japanese soldiers did not carry a debt. On average, comfort women would receive around 1,500¥ ($14.13) per month, thus devoting 750¥ to their assigned master. The food and material they were provided came at a cost, and their prices were grossly inflated to increase the master's profit. In 1943, the Japanese Army issued mandates to withhold the women who could not pay back their debts so that they were unable to return home even after the war.[25]

Due to the lack of official documentation, as much of it was falsified and destroyed, the number of comfort women during this seven-year period from 1938 to 1945 is difficult to estimate. It is approximated to be between 200,000 and 410,000 women. In 1993, the UN Tribunal on Violations of Women's Human Rights estimated that by the end of the Second World War, 90 percent of these women had died.[26] During the final stand of Japanese military forces in 1944–45, the schematic solution to ensure that this aspect of military operations was concealed was to ensure that these women died, whether it was through forcing them commit suicide or having the military kill them.

In one such event, seventy women were killed in a mistaken expected American assault. The Japanese occupying the region had already been convinced through government propaganda that the Anglo-Americans were "white devils"[27] who practiced cannibalism—their favorite food allegedly being Asians. This propaganda was believed by the comfort women, which led to many of them choosing death by suicide over the assumed future terror. Thus, during the Battle of Saipan (in the Northern Mariana Islands), women jumped off the cliffs of Saipan.

After the war, the women who survived the horrors of working in comfort stations were faced with many challenges—confronting not only the physical and psychological devastation wrought from years of sexual enslavement but also the social aspect of trying to integrate back into regular, albeit ravaged, postwar society.

Near the end of the war in 1945, when Kim found herself stationed in Singapore, the Japanese forces began to transfer women out of the brothels in order to have them work as nurses. While waiting for rescue, she was doing the work that was initially promised to many of the girls. She did not know that she was doing this because the Japanese army was refusing to admit defeat, keeping the girls working care jobs for a year after the war had ended. It was only when Allied forces demanded that the hospitals be closed that the women were finally released. Eight years after her abduction from Korea, in 1947, Kim returned home.

The years of sexual enslavement were not something she could even begin to explain to her family. They believed that she had been working in a factory for all that time. Yet as Kim got older and was challenged by many, particularly her mother, as to why she was not married yet, she finally confessed what had really happened—the realities of what had been done and the abuse that had marred her body. She thought that she had to keep this problem to herself and avoid ruining a man's life through marriage. After the horrifying discovery of her daughter's history and the realization that she also could not talk about it publicly, her mother died from a heart attack, which Kim believed to have been a direct result of sharing her secret.[28]

Eventually, Kim moved to Busan, where her sisters lived, and operated a successful restaurant. She met a man there whom she fell deeply in love with, but she was never able to have a child because of the damage done to her body. She held on to the secret of her past throughout her marriage, and when her husband eventually passed away, he died without knowing what had really happened to her during the war. It was not until after his death that she finally decided to speak out about her experience. Kim subsequently worked as an activist through her foundation, the Butterfly Fund, and through her artwork, which imparted her experiences and memories of childhood. She became a leader and spokesperson of the comfort woman movement, using the remainder of her life to support other victims and advocate for justice. Kim Bok-dong passed away in a Seoul, South Korea, hospital in January 2019.

In Confucian cultures like that of Korea, Japan, and China, where the idea of premarital sex is laden with deep shame, the issue of comfort women has been ignored, trivialized, discredited, and condemned for decades. Within such cultures, there is a tradition that a woman who loses her virginity before marriage is destined for suicide, and if she chooses to live, she willingly makes herself a social outcast. These women become social pariahs, denigrated for their lack of chastity. Consequently, comfort women were silenced and disparaged through society, media, and politics.

During the mid- to late 1980s, when the Republic of South Korea became a liberal democracy, women began to speak publicly about what happened to them. The Japanese government continued to argue that the recruitment of comfort women was nothing more than a form of licensed prostitution and that these women were there through their own consent. Then in 1993, after much public criticism and demand, the Japanese government finally acknowledged the atrocity. After polarizing and controversial debates, the women received 5 million yen ($42,000 USD) in compensation through unofficial private donations rather than through the government, with a signed letter of apology by Prime Minister Tomiichi Murayama.[29] The majority of these women found the apology and the compensation insincere, belittling, and nullifying of the issue at hand. The unofficial nature of the donations confirmed how they were erased from society and history. So many survivors of sexual exploitation could never return home due to the shame that fell upon them. They were invisible in society, politics, and religion. They did not receive justice, and the Japanese government was not held accountable for its war crimes.

In 2015, when South Korea asked for a stronger apology—after other social events illuminated what had transpired—Japan condemned the request, as they believed their past apology had been sufficient. The stance was indicative of their attitude toward the issue. They distorted the narratives, taking measures to destroy some evidence while overstating other pieces of information, and ultimately stripped any truth from these women's stories—solidifying this piece of history as an ongoing, though largely condemned, controversy in Japan.

While the treatment of comfort women has been oversimplified to criticize only the Japanese government and military, the issue is far more complex, involving the participation of Korean society as well. The hostility between the two nations reveals the polarized exchange concerning the issue of sexualized young women. Japan worked to devalue the significance of the individual and collective social psychology in coping with the obscene cruelty inflicted upon the comfort women—women whose pain, integrity, and narratives became entangled in the polarity of political-economic power and traditions of patriarchy.

In the comfort women's struggle to survive, they endured shame, abandonment, poverty, and physical and psychological pain, as Korean society wasn't prepared to hear their stories and the Japanese government kept denying the atrocities. Both countries contributed to the invisibility of these women who suffered grave consequences during the war. As women's voices are silenced and their experiences are erased, the path toward healing becomes obstructed, and women become further invisible in society, among family, and in the home.

Sharing Stories to Become Visible and Vocal

Though Asian American women may not remember or have access to the generations of pain that preceded them, bred them, and sculpted the world in which they live, it remains in the shadows of their identities and the very blood of their veins.

Asian Americans today have to fight for recognition of their cultural importance and social presence. We need only to look to our mothers, our grandmothers, and all the women who came before to recognize that while sacrifice is central to Asian American culture, to the Confucian filial ideal, sacrifice is intrinsic to the Asian woman's life.

The Asian women in our history did not have the privilege to question tradition. They did not have the opportunity to challenge the institution. They simply lived in hope of seeing the next day, surviving in a world that devalued them, and perhaps even finding happiness. But their efforts, and more importantly, their stories, have too often been hidden and left unshared. We must share and rediscover our history. This is essential to the development of the Asian American cultural consciousness.

What unifies living generations of Asian American women is a type of verbal deficiency, an absent vocabulary—a chronicle of shared stories that might indicate where we have come from, where we are going, and what it means to feel whole. The events and culture of the past, though the names and faces change, work collectively to keep Asian American women invisible.

2

IMMIGRATION

Old Doors, New Doors

North America is a land of immigrants. Other than Indigenous Peoples, everyone is either an immigrant or a descendant of immigrants. The first white European immigrants perceived themselves as the conquerors and new rulers of this novel, expansive geography. Retrospectively, the dark legacies of enslaved Africans, Asian indentured workers, and Central American migrant workers and the exploitation and genocide of Indigenous Peoples, reveal a pattern of European domination and supremacy over Native and emerging ethnic communities. Because of this legacy and the way in which white supremacy is ingrained in North American societies and institutions, Asian immigrants' struggle to make a new start was and still is overshadowed by discrimination.

Asian migration to North America began in the 1500s.[1] Out of desperation, a small number of Asian migrants left their native countries to find work, only to discover strenuous and life-threatening alternatives in their new countries. Asia and the Americas first became connected through European colonization and global trade after Columbus embarked on his search for Asia and instead came to America. European colonization on both sides of the Pacific Ocean led to the first migration of Asians to the Americas.[2] In the sixteenth century, Spanish trading ships known as Manila galleons brought Asian sailors, slaves, and servants (primarily men) to present-day Mexico as part of the creation of Spain's Pacific empire. Subjected to vermin and filth, half of those on board died during the journey. With the poor travel conditions, those who migrated and survived never traveled across the Pacific again, ultimately coming to settle and marry local women.[3]

In the nineteenth century, Americans went to Asia in search of trade and investments. The trading vessels gave way to massive transpacific steamships that soon brought Asian goods and laborers to the United States. American labor recruiters and transportation companies encouraged and facilitated Asian immigration into the early twentieth century. Immigration to the United States became an economic lifeline for many families on both sides of the Pacific Ocean.[4] In Asia, it was usually a man who left for America to work and send money back to his family. In the United States, Asian laborers were cheap and did difficult and often life-threatening work that was not done by any other ethnic group. Therefore, both groups benefited from Asian workers in America.

In the early 1900s, US colonial and military occupations and engagements in the Philippines, Japan, Korea, and Southeast Asia also impacted immigration, as it brought Asians to the United States as military brides, adoptees, and refugees.[5] To Americans, the very word *Asian* has been typically limited to East Asians; however, the term encompasses diverse peoples across Southeast Asia, South Asia, and the Pacific Islands who make up a diverse Asian American community.[6]

Asians came to the United States as temporary employees and migrant workers and eventually became indentured workers who lost most of their freedom. Indentured laborers toiled long hours to pay back the money they borrowed to come to America. They were in so much debt, they couldn't buy land or homes or even obtain the right to vote, as they were prohibited from obtaining American citizenship. Indentured workers lived in dismal conditions, enduring the indignities of discrimination and racism as invisible noncitizens.

The Chinese first immigrated to the United States for employment opportunities. Many fled overcrowded urban centers following the collapse of the peasant economy in China. America had a high demand for cheap labor and the lure of California gold after 1849. Many also migrated for work in the sugarcane plantations of Hawaii and in the "Gold Mountains" (*Gam Saan*) of California. Many laborers in California were initially involved in mining and railroad construction and later in manufacturing, agriculture, and land reclamation.[7]

The Burlingame-Seward Treaty (1868) permitted the legal migration of unskilled laborers from China to the United States to fill the void of cheap laborers. This treaty eased immigration restrictions and limited American interference in internal Chinese affairs. There was a steady flow of Chinese labor for American companies. But this treaty was short lived, as by the 1870s, there was an increase in anti-Chinese sentiment aimed at stopping the migration of Chinese laborers.[8]

Through American recruitment and volition, Chinese immigrants were brought in as coolies to replace slaves in the plantation fields after the Civil War. They also performed the dangerous tasks of drilling dynamite and laying out the tracks for the first transcontinental railroad. Three Chinese laborers died for every two miles of track, but when the celebratory photo of the golden spike was taken at the railroad's completion, not a single Chinese man was welcomed to pose with the other—white—railway workers.[9] These Chinese coolies were expendable, doing some of the most hazardous jobs without compensation. They built some of the longest and most arduous stretches of the railroad by boring tunnels through the granite rocks of the Sierra Nevada and by laying tracks across the deserts of Nevada and Utah. At the peak of its construction in 1868, the Central Pacific Railroad employed more than twelve thousand Chinese laborers. They were efficient and diligent workers who toiled for lower wages than others. However, xenophobia and fear that the Chinese might populate California prohibited the Chinese indentured workers from bringing their wives or family members, whereas European immigrants were able to take their wives and families with them as they moved.[10]

Similar to the present rhetoric about immigrants "taking jobs," even then, Asian immigrants were chastised for taking away work from white Americans. However, they were simply meeting the demand for cheap—at times, free—labor. They came to the United States and sought to make enough money to return to Asia. But as these men worked, they realized they would never be able to earn enough and ended up remaining in the United States. As indentured workers, they didn't have much freedom to move, seek different employment, marry, or buy property without permission from their employer. They were indentured with payment for their passage.[11] They silently endured many hardships for the sake of their families back home and for their own futures in the United States.

Chinese immigration in the 1850s to California was soon followed by the migration of Japanese (1880s), Korean (1903), and Filipino (1990) workers to Hawaii, which became the fiftieth US state in 1959. These groups of migrants were expected to contribute to American projects yet were consistently exploited and abused. Racism and fear of Chinese workers led to a foreign miners' license tax, which required every foreign miner to pay a monthly tax of three dollars. The tax was aimed at Chinese laborers, who were ineligible to become American citizens, as the Naturalization Act of 1790 reserved this privilege for "free white persons" who had lived in the United States for at least two years. It excluded indentured servants, slaves, and most women. Black and Asian immigrants were not eligible to be naturalized. Later nineteenth-century legislation still included a racial requirement for citizenship.[12] These discriminatory laws and practices against people of color continued to penalize Chinese workers with taxes despite their work as indentured servants.

Women and Immigration

At the beginning of Asian immigration, only a small percentage of women migrated. Those who did were often viewed as prostitutes if they were not married. Seen as seductresses, bound to the stereotypes of dragon ladies, a view of East Asian women as cunning, deceitful, and domineering, or lotus blossoms, a view of East Asian women as objects of explicit sexual appeal or commodification, Asian women are constructed through art and literature as obedient, exotic beings who existed to merely fulfill a white male sexual fantasy. This can be seen in the prevalence of Asian women in pornography, the rise of mail-order brides from Southeast Asia, the Asian fetish, and sexual violence against Asian women.[13]

Some early Asian women immigrants did not expect to remain in their new countries permanently or obtain citizenship. Some Chinese girls were brought to the United States as young as fifteen years old; many of them were abducted and smuggled into the country. They were locked in a boardinghouse to be raped ten times a day until they contracted syphilis and were discarded, dumped out on the streets to die alone.[14] Besides these young girls, some Asian women were allowed to immigrate to Hawaii in part because it was an American colony (it became a state in 1959) with only a small percentage of whites. Some of the Asian women's drive for immigration to the United States was largely prompted by the rising desire for social freedom; however, oftentimes their migration was more sinisterly arranged and orchestrated by men promising security who only used them for their own profit and sexual exploitation.[15]

Later, the demand for new Asian workers rose. Subsequently, the demand for Asian women rose to balance the gender gap. Women in the migrating communities of the early 1900s were imported from their homelands out of the traditional, patriarchal need to have women serve men and carry on the family lineage by giving birth to sons. Patriarchal standards thus continued in a new foreign context: the insulated Asian diasporas of America.

Many Asian women were gravely misinformed about life in the United States, carrying dreamy expectations that would soon be dismantled. When they arrived, they faced the brutal reality of sordid living conditions in a place that had not seen many faces like theirs. There was little chance of returning to their countries of origin, so they had to find any means they could to survive. While some women worked in the fields as part of the plantation workforce, others were employed in immigrant camps to cook food and to mend and wash clothes.

Legal Discrimination

During the 1860s and 1870s, hostility toward Asian workers in the United States intensified with the formation of organizations such as the Asiatic Exclusion League. Chinese Americans in particular, who composed the majority of the Asian population on the mainland, were viewed as the "Yellow Peril" and suffered intense discrimination and violence, culminating in lynchings and large-scale assaults. In 1875, Congress passed the first restrictive immigration law against Asian Americans: the Page Act. This recognized forced Asian laborers and Asian women (whom the law assumed might engage in prostitution) as "undesirables" who would be barred from entering the United States. In practice, the law led to a nearly complete exclusion of Chinese women from entering the country, preventing male Asian immigrants from bringing their families with or after them.[16]

The Page Act was passed with the intention to keep cheap Chinese labor out of the United States. The law also regulated the entry of Chinese women, as a growing population of Americans feared that the presence of Asian women would lead to the birth of a second generation of Asians in the United States.[17] There were anti-Chinese campaigns after the mid-1800s that resulted in Chinese immigrants being unable to leave their homes without being spat at, clubbed, or shot in the back. In the 1880s, the fear of a "Chinese invasion" was born, stemming from the outgrowth of the anti-Chinese sentiment that had been brewing. People were so fearful of the Chinese overrunning America that politicians eventually pursued the lawful prevention of Chinese immigration.[18]

Throughout this period, Chinese immigrants in the United States were vulnerable to ethnic cleansing. Vigilantes planted bombs in their businesses, shot them through tents, and smoked them out of their homes. Along the West Coast, thousands of Chinese immigrants were driven out of their towns. In 1885, several white men broke into a Tacoma, Washington, home and accosted a pregnant woman. They dragged her outside by her hair and forced her to march, along with three hundred other Chinese immigrants in town, out into the cold, rainy night as their homes were set on fire and burned behind them.[19]

The fear of the Chinese invasion eventually led to the Chinese Exclusion Act of 1882. This act was the first immigration law to ban a race of people from entering the United States. It came after legislators and media characterized the Chinese as "rats" and "lepers" but also "machine-like" workers who stole jobs from "good white Americans."[20] The Chinese Exclusion Act forbade immigration from China to the United States, denied naturalization of Chinese immigrants already in the United States, and denied citizenship to American-born children of Chinese immigrants. This denial of citizenship actually went against the Fourteenth Amendment (1870), which guarantees citizenship to all children born in the United States. But the 1882 act made Chinese children an exception to the rule.[21] This denial of citizenship has not been experienced by any other ethnic group in American history. Similarly, in Canada, legislators passed the Chinese Immigration Act (1923), which completely prohibited the Chinese from immigrating to Canada. It was repealed on May 14, 1947.

In 1917, the US government expanded the ban to all of Asia, later even restricting Filipinos from coming in, even though the Philippines was a former US colony. The immigration ban was racial segregation on a global scale. The Chinese Exclusion Act also placed new restrictions on Chinese people who already lived in the United States. They had to obtain certifications to reenter the country if they ever left to visit family. The courts could deport them at any time, which broke up families and communities. When the Chinese Exclusion Act expired in 1892, Congress extended it for another ten years through the Geary Act. This was then made permanent in 1902, requiring Chinese residents to register and obtain a certificate of residence. Without a certificate, they faced up to one year of hard labor followed by deportation. This act, which was supposed to last only ten years, was extended all the way to 1943.

Congress finally repealed the exclusion acts in 1943 and allowed 105 foreign-born Chinese a year to seek naturalization. In 1943, the Chinese were finally allowed to become US citizens, and as a result, they were allowed to vote.[22] The devastating act of 1882 lasted sixty-one years and created pain and suffering not only for the Chinese but also for other Asian Americans, as discrimination was extended to those who looked racially similar to the Chinese.

During the early twentieth century, various laws were implemented to stop the flow of Asian immigrants to the United States. Anti-Asian sentiments from the nineteenth century led to the National Origins Act of 1924, which prohibited Asians from immigrating to the United States because they were seen as a threat. While Northern European countries were allowed to send immigrants of both genders into the United States, the 1924 act prohibited women from China, Japan, Korea, and India from entering the United States, even as wives of US citizens. This law was not changed until 1945 with the passage of the War Brides Act, which allowed the immigration of Asian spouses and children of US servicemen. However, Asians living in the United States were not allowed to become naturalized citizens until the McCarren-Walter Act of 1952. These laws and acts revealed white America's discriminatory attitudes toward Asians, which clearly impacted the livelihood and psychology of Asian Americans. They were a form of racism based on a conservative political philosophy that claimed the need for classes in a well-ordered society.

In 1965, the Immigration and Nationality Act abolished the national origins formula that had been in place since 1924. Signed into law by President Johnson, the Immigration and Nationality Act terminated national origins quotas and instead created an annual limitation of twenty thousand visas per country (in this law, Taiwan and Mainland China were considered as one origin). Those with skills and family in the United States were granted priority. Thus, since the mid-1960s, the Chinese have immigrated to the United States in significant numbers, taking advantage of the immigration policy's emphasis on family reunification.[23]

When Americans welcomed the Chinese back in 1965, it was also on account of their entanglement in an ideological contest with the Soviet Union. Earlier that year, the United States had a major public relations issue, and if they were going to stamp out the tide of communism in poor non-Western countries, they had to reboot their racist Jim Crow image and prove that their democracy was superior. The Chinese would help the dominant white society.

During this time, the model minority myth was popularized to keep communists—and Black people—in check. Asian American success was circulated to promote capitalism and to undermine the credibility of Black civil rights. Asian Americans were presented as the "good ones," since they were undemanding, diligent workers who were generalized as never asking for handouts from the government. They did not face discrimination as long as they were deemed compliant and hardworking.[24] There was reason for white Americans to want different racialized groups to be in conflict with one another, a situation that only reinforced white superiority and power.

Asian exclusion laws had a global impact. Anti-Asian racism moved across national boundaries and contributed to an emerging worldwide system of immigration regulation. By the early twentieth century, the United States had set the terms and logic of the "Asian immigration problem" that nearly every country in the western hemisphere, from Canada to Argentina, adopted or adapted to. During World War II, these policies merged with new concerns about national and hemispheric security. Japanese Americans were uprooted from their homes and incarcerated in the name of "military necessity." Similarly, Japanese Canadians were sent into exile, and Japanese Latin Americans faced restrictions in their daily lives—some were even expelled.[25] The effects of these policies often go unnoticed today, but many still view Asian immigrants with suspicion, albeit less obvious.

These early immigration actions are indicative of systemic racism toward Asian Americans, who were still attempting to enter the country and were not yet citizens. In 1965, Asian Americans were given some parity with European immigrants with the Immigration and Nationality Act, by which national origin was removed as a criterion for immigration into the country. But lasting fears about Asian Americans still emerge today.

Hawaii and California

Between 1850 and 1920, over three hundred thousand Asians traveled to Hawaii. Some of the Chinese joined the first workers in the Hawaiian sugar industry and helped transform it into a "king" industry while at the same time displacing Native Hawaiian laborers.[26]

Asian immigrants were at times called "sojourners" (e.g., international students and indentured laborers/coolies), and others who integrated as settlers (e.g., paper sons and picture brides[27]) worked in the plantations of Hawaii; the fisheries of Alaska and Louisiana; the railroads, gold mines, farms, and gardens of the West; and the industrialized agribusiness sites of the Midwest. Despite individual and collective endeavors to perform what Kimberly McKee calls "cultural whiteness," Asian Americans were disenfranchised as racially other and segregated as not-quite-white throughout US history and popular culture. The "ethnic" sense of being Filipino, Chinese, Japanese, Indian, Korean, or Vietnamese American was reified through colonial encounters in Asia and changing US immigration and settlement policies. The Supreme Court in the early 1900s categorized Asians in the United States as "nonwhite" despite their generally pale skin, patriotic military service, decades of residency, English fluency, American education, and Christianity. Laws and hegemonic discourses of the United States have kept Asian immigrants on the periphery, so it is no wonder that many Asian Americans believe that their ancestors' historic contributions to the United States have been made "invisible."[28]

Korean Immigration

Korean immigration patterns differed from other Asian groups, as many Koreans initially did not want to immigrate to the United States. Missionaries played an active role in reducing the initial resistance to the idea of immigration. In the early 1900s, a number of American missionaries persuaded members of their congregations to go to Hawaii, a Christian land. As a result of the active role missionaries played, an estimated 40 percent of the seven thousand emigrants who left the country between December 1902 and May 1905 were converts to Christianity. Unlike the Chinese and Japanese, who came from geographically confined areas, Korean emigrants originated from many places, especially seaports and their vicinities. Furthermore, few Korean immigrants came from agricultural backgrounds. Of the seven thousand Koreans taken to Hawaii, about one thousand eventually returned home, while another thousand proceeded to the mainland.[29] Those who returned home realized that America was not the land of "milk and honey" as white American missionaries had told them; rather, it was a place immersed in racial tension.

At the camps and plantations, Korean women worked in slave-like conditions. They weeded, stripped leaves, and harvested the same as the men but were paid significantly less. Then after working in the fields, women cooked, washed, and cleaned not only for their own families but often—for a small fee—for the bachelors and married men who had come without their wives. Those who cooked for single men had to get up at three or four in the morning to make breakfast and boxed lunches for as many as forty people.[30] Others who worked in the fields for wages spent a full day under the sun, sometimes with babies strapped to their backs, before returning home to fix supper. In the evenings, they washed, ironed, and mended. Those who bore children did all this work while also being pregnant.[31] All the while, through the physical exhaustion of constant labor, Asian American women grappled with the deep psychological hardships and discriminatory legislation.

After the Korean War, many South Koreans lived in poverty. The country was divided into North Korea and South Korea, leaving the nation devastated, as the population endured the forced separation of families, friends, and communities. Facing social and economic devastation at home, the Korean people sought refuge from the bleakness of their home country. Desperate young Korean families during the 1970s went in search of better opportunities in North America.

Furthermore, an amendment to the 1965 Immigration and Nationality Act abolished the earlier quota system based on national origin and established a new immigration policy based on reuniting immigrant families and attracting skilled laborers to the United States. Therefore, when the 1965 immigration ban was lifted by the United States, many Asian families decided to immigrate. Only select professionals from Asia were granted visas to the United States: doctors, engineers, and mechanics. This screening process gave rise to the model minority myth. The US government only allowed the most educated and highly experienced Asians, using their success as the faulty paradigm for all other struggling immigrants while trivializing Asians' concerns. The dominant society could then claim that anyone could live the American dream while they pointed to Asian immigrants, the vast majority of whom came into the country as highly educated working professionals such as doctors, scientists, and engineers.[32]

Korean American Women's Identity and the Church

Korean North American women feel pressure to preserve their Korean cultural heritage and to assimilate into Western sociocultural realities in order to survive. Upon their arrival in North America, their identities were in flux. In Korea, many women never had the opportunity to fully experiment with, challenge, and explore their senses of self. After immigration, their new environment prompted them to search for the path to self-realization and self-fulfillment that they could not claim in their youth. Many Korean immigrant women started to work outside the home. Even though they experienced racism, their jobs created spaces for self-reflection and growth that proved to be life-giving. Personal histories and family ties that traditionally formed women's self-image were quickly confronted with a polarizing North American reality. They were suddenly able to view themselves as separate from their families and able to nurture their own self-identity.

Still, Korean American women's lives are pushed to the margins of white society, going on to experience sexism in the church, a community haven for Korean immigrants. Korean American women straddle both cultures—not only linguistically but also culturally, religiously, and socially. They must live a life balanced on two opposing spectrums and worlds. For example, I was expected to speak Korean at home and English outside the home. This was not easy, as my limited Korean language skills led me to feel shame when I could not converse with my family members. Furthermore, I was exposed to Korean culture, history, and philosophy through my parents, church, and Korean language school. My parents expected me to learn about North American wars, leaders, and important events as well as Korean history. As I tried my best to straddle the western and eastern worlds, I felt myself living with enormous tension as I fumbled to accommodate two conflicting cultures. Afraid of letting down my parents, who struggled to create a life for our family, I fumbled my way, often unsuccessfully, through assimilating into white culture. I often felt exhausted, torn, and duplicitous.

My experience is echoed in the accounts of many women who share my racial and cultural background. As Korean American women try to live in between cultures and achieve a complicated balance, they often find themselves in liminal spaces. Existing in these spaces prevents Korean American women from coming to the center of the dominant culture, as they are continuously pushed out into the margins of society. They are always perceived as foreigners and therefore cannot be viewed as "true" Americans. As perpetual foreigners, they do not find belonging in either community. Furthermore, patriarchal Korean cultural norms push women aside and further marginalize them. Therefore, Korean American women experience oppression and marginalization from white culture as well as from their Korean culture.

The Korean American community has high expectations of maintaining one's language, culture, heritage, and history. There is an expectation that younger immigrant children and the generations that follow will carry on the Korean heritage and culture. This push-and-pull existence of being in between cultures and rejected from the center creates psychological tension. For Korean American women, the extra layer of patriarchy adds an unnecessary physical and mental burden, as it requires additional navigation and negotiations to survive. Being on the margins results in an identity of marginality.

Korean American women do not come to live on the margins by choice but are forced into this existence. Korean American women feel this, even as members of second, third, or fourth generations that continue to live in America. White society still does not fully accept Korean American women as part of the dominant society, as they are made out to be perpetual foreigners. On the one hand, they can never speak English well enough to appease Americans; on the other hand, they cannot be fully accepted into Korean culture because they speak Korean with an American accent. Some members of the Korean community often comment that Korean American women who are independent and career oriented are too westernized and therefore not truly Korean.

Korean American women also exist within an Asian American subculture where the expectations among different Asian cultures clash. When a Chinese American woman marries a Korean American man, the two subcultures are in conflict because they have different expectations of women. In addition to being members of a marginalized Asian American subculture that functions with rules the majority does not live by, Korean American women often experience the frustration of not having their experience recognized, validated, and supported by men within their own ethnic communities. Thus they are doubly alienated: they experience alienation from within their ethnic community and from the broader North American culture.[33] These women's experiences are limited and constrained to a small, stifling ethnocentric circle.

Furthermore, just as in Korea, a person's identity in this ethnic circle is defined not only by themselves but by others around them, especially family members. Although transplanted to North American soil, Korean American women's expressions of individuality lack the marks of individuality as defined by the dominant North American culture. Rather, the Confucian identity of a woman is transferred to the North American identity. For example, in Korean communities, all women are addressed in terms of their family relationships (or lack thereof). If married, a woman's full name becomes obsolete, and people call her "Mrs." or "So-and-so's wife." If a woman has a child or children, she is referred to as the mother of her firstborn. The only time a woman's full name is recognized and used is when she is relatively young and unmarried (approximately twenty-five years and younger). After a certain age (approximately twenty-six years old), an unmarried woman is often recognized as a *no-chea-nyeu* (old maid).[34] Similar to most cultures, an older, unmarried woman is looked down upon, just as they were during the Confucian era.

My Family's Story

My family fit into the significant wave of Asian immigration in the 1970s. Postwar Korea saw many young families leave in hopes of better economic prospects and social freedoms in North America; however, this new life came at a cost. Lofty dreams of freedom, opportunity, and novelty were shadowed by heavy socioeconomic barriers, cultural dissidence, and racial discrimination.

Unsettled by the undercurrent of anguish that captured my family after immigration, like most other Asians of my time and before, I did my best to overcome it by aiming for success, which meant becoming part of white society. Little by little, I started to learn to fit in—frequently failing but trying nonetheless. The more I adapted to the blueprint of white society, the more I began to feel closer to those in the outside world. However, in the midst of my "white awakening," I continued to lose touch with the fragmented core of my Asian identity.

Losing Our Identities

The general perception of Asians in North American society made Asian Americans feel the need to diminish their heritage, language, culture, and history for smoother assimilation. Through various forms of racism and discrimination, Asian identities became not only nexuses of shame and insecurity but also obstructions to entry into "regular" society with all of its benefits. The new Asian immigrants quickly realized that in order to get ahead, they had to do their best to become more like the white society around them. Their native Asian names were slowly erased along with their languages, cultures, and native traditions.

Much of my formation as a child took place in the tension between preserving my Asian culture in an ethnic ghetto and conforming to a North American culture in my schooling. I felt like two separate people as I adhered to different ways of being in the two distinct cultures. At home and at church, I spoke Korean and acted like a Korean. I lived in complete obedience to my parents and elders. In North American culture, I tried to shed my Koreanness as much as possible by speaking in English and trying to act like the rest of the white kids at church. But as much as I tried, I could never completely eradicate the traces of my Korean upbringing. In the end, both halves of my identity got so lost in self-scrutiny that they eventually dissipated into nothing. I felt myself become invisible.

In the eyes of some, Asian Americans are more defined by the "Asian" aspect than the "American" one; but in the eyes of others, Asian Americans are "probationary" Americans, existing as if they are auditioning for the role. Even after multiple generations of living in the United States, Asian Americans are still not fully accepted as Americans. They remain on the outside, living in the invisible peripheries of dominant spaces, not just marginalized by racial oppression and discrimination around them but also marginalized by a subversive, communal will to live peacefully, even prosperously, in a country with extensive roots in white supremacy.

Thus, if Asian Americans occasionally fall silent when confronted with racism and seem to work harder to gain success, it is not because they desire to be model minorities but because this title has been thrust upon them. This stereotype has prevented many Asian Americans from speaking out against racism, social injustices, and prejudices—though many of them are not aware of this dynamic. Asian American invisibility is a result not of our own cultural barriers and perceived meekness, but of our dissonant collective psyche instigated by the erasure of our cultural identity from the dominant society.[35]

The Pain of Leaving and the Hope of Arriving

My paternal grandmother gave her assets and savings to each of her sons as they got married, allocating the largest amount to her oldest son, my uncle. My father used his share to buy his first home in Korea. The residence was an anomaly in our little suburban neighborhood; spacious and light filled, it was a beautiful home that was markedly larger, brighter, and newer than the typical homes around us. Unlike those other houses however, which had front yards designated for an outhouse and laundry, our front yard was for leisurely recreation. Our little dog, who my father named Happy, ran around a yard with a well-maintained garden full of an abundance of medicinal herbs and vegetables my mother grew. An aviary at the front of our home looked out into the yard and housed yellow canaries and manicured mini bonsais edged by windows. In those early years, everything my father enjoyed, we as a family were able to enjoy too.

Yet, we left it all behind when we immigrated. My father sold our lovely home in exchange for a single room in a house with another family. It was an apparent downgrade, but my older sister and I didn't care. She was five and I was four, and we were completely unaware of the monumental shift in the quality of our surroundings. We felt that the tiny new place was a playground. That temporary room—our home until we left for Canada—had a small attic for storage. We often played make-believe in the attic, swinging open the door and pretending that it was a bus door. There, on the bus, the attendant would call out the various stops for the passengers and collect the fare. We role-played as passengers and attendants, calling out invented stops in invented lands. It was the fantasy ride to our next destination, the future move across the world in the back of our minds. Swinging the door one last time, we eventually reached the day of our departure. This time, the bus would not pick us up again.

On our final day in Korea, my extended family organized a large gathering, where all my aunts, uncles, and cousins came together for one final celebration. It seemed as though there was always an occasion to get together, so this was a wonderfully familiar way to say goodbye to our life in Korea.

I remember eating until I couldn't eat anymore, talking until I couldn't talk anymore, and playing until I couldn't stay awake any longer. My parents' farewells were brief as they tried to get my sister and me home and rested for the next day. I left with the idea that I would see my family again soon, seeing as how our goodbyes were done without the knowledge that we were leaving them behind. After all, I did not understand precisely what we would be leaving behind—family, friends, language, home, comfort, love—and for how long.

I later learned that when my father announced his plans for departure to his mother, she wept uncontrollably. She believed that she would never see her son or granddaughters again. Unbeknown to me at the time, my mother also believed we would never see our extended family again. We were walking off into the unknown. Koreans were just beginning to migrate in larger numbers to North America; immigrants and their families did not know how often they would be able to return home or how their new country would change them.

My grandmother was not only heartbroken by my parents' decision to leave Korea but terrified by the idea of her son trying to survive in a new country while supporting a young family. She contributed more and more to his savings, knowing he struggled with financial competency and job security. While my father was gifted academically, he lacked practical knowledge and skills, and he was showing the beginnings of psychological instability.

In the 1970s, before the internet became available, the fastest communication was via telephone. Even so, telephones were costly and slow; we could only make a few international calls a year, and there was always an audio lag that felt like an eternity before we could finally hear a loved one over the background noise.

At the airport, my grandmother watched us walk away with our stuffed red luggage, down the jetway to the plane. I remember her crying, curling into herself as she looked out at my sister and me. We looked back, taking a final glance at her. I remember thinking it would only be a short while before I saw her again as I stepped onto the plane.

When I recall my last days in Korea, I fall into a strange feeling. The memories transport me to a time of heightened emotions and expectations, feeling my family's excitement, sadness, fear, regret, and hope. We were so full of ambition and innocence, expressed with the purest hope to do better and *be* better—not knowing how the future would resist us. This is the story of Asian immigrants: the story of hoping, fighting, laboring, sacrificing, and remaining for the belief that you won't just survive against all odds but thrive gloriously.

Dreams Dashed and Racism Endured

In the face of widespread social and economic devastation in Korea after the war, my father, like many other Koreans, sought to move to North America to find new opportunities. Though not yet a religious man, my father heard from numerous American and Canadian missionaries working in Korea of the booming employment in their countries. He fell deep into romantic notions of American prosperity—big homes and large green backyards—and longed to be free of the suffering and poverty that pervaded postwar Korea.

When my family immigrated to Canada, nothing could have prepared us for the life that lay ahead. Right away, my parents found their financial, cultural, and social status altered in the foreign environment. Our difficulties were contained in our Asian American communities, our homes, and our minds, internalized into a collective insecurity that the outside world turned away from and pretended not to notice.

When Asians migrated in waves to North America during the 1960s and 1970s, there was a unified sense of disappointment in the life that awaited them, which was pervaded by racial discrimination, xenophobia, and social isolation. The situation called for sacrifice and indemnity, suffering and redemptive success—elements that were already present in many Confucian Asian cultures.

In 1975, my family came to Canada in the middle of Toronto's cold, harsh winter. Everything from my naïve, early understanding of the world was erased in this foreign land. Things that were once so ordinary to me—people, language, nature, buildings, food—disappeared and were instead replaced by a strange, cold vastness.

Many Asians immigrated to Toronto in the 1970s. They entered a space in which they were had not yet been commonly encountered and therefore not yet valued for any real purpose. The fluctuations of racial awareness and social correctness that prevail today had not yet hit their stride—a reality I was made instantly aware of as soon as we landed. At Pearson Airport, no matter which direction I looked, I saw eyes following my family, seemingly the only Asians around.

Korean immigrants dreamt of coming to North America to begin a new life with superior job opportunities, social freedoms, and large backyards, but a few days, weeks, and months after arrival, they had to immediately adjust to the reality that placed them as the outsider. Soon their dreams all vanished due to the harsh reality of daily racism and discrimination.

My mother's dream of being liberated from the cultural patriarchy and stagnant economic life was, sadly, not fulfilled. As her ability to speak English was so sparse, it was impossible for her to assimilate into Canadian society. As soon as someone tried to talk to her and realized she wouldn't be able to communicate in English, they were condescending to her. As a young girl realizing that my mother was often the subject of ridicule, I felt both mortified and infuriated. Her inability to speak English deeply impacted me, giving me the ripples of exclusion she felt on a daily basis.

There were so many things I wanted to do as a child. But I was held back by my family's circumstances, and I held myself back out of shame and isolation. A large part of the social exclusion I faced wasn't just racial but economic. As a result, I grew up with deep resentment against other poor kids like me because I was poor, and I hated it. The land of milk and honey was not for my family—at least not, then. Our residence for nearly a decade was the Frontenac Apartments complex in London, Ontario. It was the proverbial, run-down, bug-infested hole in the wall. We had two bedrooms and one bath. It was not a place to invite friends over, nor was it a place I found homey and pleasant. Without any extended family, my sister and I began to feel isolation creeping in—just like the cold that forced us to bundle up in our jackets and blankets on the floor of our little apartment.

My dad could not hold a job for long. There were many reasons for this; primarily, his health was never good. He would get sick because of something that he ate, getting indigestion, feeling weak, and lying in his bedroom all day, unable to get up. He would miss work frequently because of this and would subsequently get fired just as often. In one of his more stable jobs at the GM Motors assembly line, he was laid off for months at a time for various reasons. We often lived on unemployment checks during times of his bad health.

My father was also not one to splurge on our family. We slept on used mattresses or simply on the floor during the warmer months for many years. My mother finally saved enough money to buy my sister and me new beds. Though they were cheap, I remember squealing with delight at the thought of sleeping so high off the ground, just like white people slept on TV. My mother bought them without telling our father, so when the new beds arrived, he was livid, declaring that none of us would get to even touch them because he would return them immediately. When he started lying down and eventually realizing how comfortable the mattress was, we took it as authorization that we could keep it.

There were eight Korean families in our apartment complex. Some of them we knew and became friendly with, while others were near strangers and even more closed off than we were. Over the years, they each moved out of the building one by one. We lived there the longest, staying there for a total of nine years.

Immigrating in the winter proved to be more difficult than my parents had imagined. After our first two weeks in Toronto, we moved to London, Ontario, in the middle of the Snow Belt, where we would live for many years at Frontenac. The snow was endless, voracious, and cruel. I disliked the snow, and even more, I dreaded the cold. The worst part of winter was walking to school. I would lie awake at night fearing the passing of time that would bring me to the next day because that meant I had to go to school and walk outside. Even then, depression took over my youth during winters. The wind lashed at my cheeks and brought tears to morning eyes as I trudged, gruelingly, through heavy snow and ice.

On one extremely cold day, I remember walking with my sister in snow so deep, it reached my knees. Just as we made it halfway to school, I realized that I had only one shoe. The other foot, numb from the cold, had only an icy, frozen sock. Dismally, I looked back at the stretch of land we had already covered and felt tears form in my eyes. I told my sister to wait where she was as I went back to find it. After searching, backtracking, and wandering in the cold, I found the pocket of snow where my shoe had fallen. As I picked it up to put it back on my foot, something seemed to grip me. I don't know what compelled me, but I put it back in the snow, then slowly took my other shoe off and laid it overtop. Now shoeless, I sat down, my feet buried and freezing underneath me. I sat there hopelessly, not wanting anyone to find me, closing my eyes and imagining time escaping altogether.

When I woke up, it was because I thought I had heard my father's aviary birds. I remembered that I had to feed them and help my mother water the plants. But when I opened my eyes to that shocking white-gray sky, I saw my sister's silhouette. She pulled me up off the ground, put my snow-filled shoes back on my feet, and jerked me by the hand back to school, muttering, "Don't tell Mom and Dad."

So much of the initial pain I felt as a young immigrant derived from a perpetual feeling of outsiderness, a sensation that convinced me I was a stranger even to myself, clinging to who I was before I left Korea and what I might have been if I had stayed. Perhaps something about this day in the snow marked the time where I fully acknowledged that the world from the past was only a memory, something that had to be left behind like shoe tracks in the snow, and the new reality I found myself in, however painful, had to be accepted as my new truth. I was reminded every day when I walked to school that there was a gap between me and the regular world—one that was far too large for me to bridge at five, ten, even twenty years old. I became indebted to the notion that I was going to constantly have to prove myself, particularly in terms of the acceptance and acknowledgment I was chasing. I know this to be inherent to the Asian American experience.

The Yellow Peril

When Asian immigrants stepped onto new soil with hopes of a better life, they were unexpectedly confronted with intense hatred and fear. Yellow Peril—the fear of immigrants from East Asia based on the misunderstanding that East Asians are an existential danger to the Western world—prevailed in white American society and culture.[36] Xenophobic at its foundation, Yellow Peril as a concept is used against Asian immigrants to cement their place as subordinates to a larger community.

Yellow Peril is not an isolated phenomenon. It is interconnected with how dominant society views and treats all people of color. For example, in the late nineteenth century, large numbers of immigrants from around the world came to the United States. Europeans commonly entered through Ellis Island in New York, where they were checked for identification, and if their documents were in order, they were registered to enter America legitimately. They waited only a couple of hours or overnight before they were allowed to enter the country. Asians, on the other hand, entered through Angel Island in San Francisco Bay, which was run like a prison.[37] Asian immigrants at Angel Island were made to wait weeks, months or even years. Rarely were European applicants sent back to their country of origin, but Asians were sent back at an alarming rate.[38] The rate at which Asians entered and remained in America is evidence of long-enduring anti-Asian sentiments as well as a growing fear of their existence in the country.

In another instance of Yellow Peril, we look toward Asian coolies—unskilled, cheap laborers. It is no coincidence that this group arrived after America abolished slavery in December 1865. As more cheap Asian laborers arrived, white fear of Asian Americans increased.

The white working class demanded that the US government halt the immigration of the Chinese, who were supposedly taking jobs. Yellow Peril racism provoked the Chinese massacre of 1871, wherein five hundred white men lynched twenty Chinese men in Chinatown in Los Angeles over a rumor that some of the Chinese had killed a white policeman. Eighteen or nineteen Chinese men were killed (10 percent of the Chinese population in Los Angeles at that time).[39] It was the largest mass lynching in American history. The street where the massacre occurred was called Calle de los Negros.[40] Even though a grand jury returned twenty-five indictments for these murders, only ten men ultimately stood trial, and only eight rioters were convicted of manslaughter. All the charges were ultimately overturned, and the defendants were never retried.[41]

Yellow Peril perhaps most gravely affected Japanese Americans. The fear of those with Japanese heritage living on the West Coast during the Second World War led to the internment of the Japanese from 1942 to 1946. Japanese Americans became security risks in the American psyche and were treated as such by the American government. Executive Order 9066, which authorized the internment of Japanese Americans, affected the lives of about 177,000 people, the majority of whom were American citizens.[42] Japanese American citizens and longtime residents lost their homes, businesses, properties, and financial savings and lived in brutal conditions in the internment camps. Those born in Japan were banned from becoming naturalized citizens until 1952, ten years after the executive order was signed and issued.

In Canada, although there is an inextricable historical connection to the restrictive US immigration policies against Asians, white supremacy wasn't something that needed to be imported across the border—not in the 1800s or the 1900s, and certainly not now. Canada has its own complex history of white nationalism, including legal discrimination such as the Head Tax on Chinese immigrants in 1885.[43] Much like it was in America, Yellow Peril was made an official policy in Canada through laws like this.

Several acts of terror in Canada against Chinese Canadians took place. In 1907, a Chinese Canadian camp near Vancouver's Coal Harbour was violently attacked by rogue groups of radicalized white nationalists.[44] Subsequently, the federal government decided that the Chinese were largely responsible for the scourge of drugs and prostitution, justifying further restrictions on Asian immigration. One measure, the 1908 continuous journey regulation, required immigrants to arrive directly—without stopovers—from their country of origin. This made it next to impossible for Asians, or any other immigrant traveling from afar, to immigrate to Canada.

After forty years of trying to ease anxieties and through systemic discrimination and foreign diplomacy, Canada gave up its moderate approach to racism and became more extreme with its own Chinese Exclusion Act in 1923—effectively banning the majority of Chinese immigration through a hefty head tax. White supremacist groups, such as White Canada Forever, celebrated; however, much of the credit can be attributed to Americans, who over the years had been pressuring Canada to ban Chinese immigrants. The Canadian Parliament repealed the act in 1947, following the proclamation of the Canadian Citizenship Act in 1946. Large-scale Chinese immigration to Canada only occurred after the liberalization of the immigration policy, which eliminated restrictions based on national origin in 1962. This was followed by the world's first points-based immigration system in 1967, which was used to screen all applicants.[45]

No Entrance

Located in London, Ontario, the Frontenac Apartments complex was a temporary place for many immigrants to live while they found a better home. There were three apartment buildings, and nearly all of the Korean immigrants lived in the middle building. The third structure had hardly any immigrants and was mainly occupied by older white folks, with the exception of one Korean family who had a daughter my age. The superintendent who worked in that apartment, an old white woman, vehemently refused to let any other Koreans into her building. In particular, she hated Korean children, who would play on the apartment grounds and go over to one another's homes frequently.

I grew to be close friends with the Korean girl who lived there, and she began to call and invite me over more often. We had to discreetly plan how I could enter the building to get to her apartment. I remember the superintendent looking out of her window all day, waiting for one of us to get too close. If the superintendent saw us walking toward the front entrance of the apartment building, she would leave her window, run to the entrance, and stand there with her arms crossed and legs splayed. She glared and shook her head, muttering angrily to herself. As a young, easily frightened kid, I would just run away. If I ever saw her face in the window after my friend invited me over, I would give up and just walk away.

The apartment building had three entrances: one at the front and one on either side of the building. My friend and I finally devised a plan for me to visit without the superintendent blocking me: She would sit by the side entrance that was farthest from the superintendent's apartment. She would wait there until I came to the side door, and then she would let me in. This way, I was undetected, as the superintendent always looked out the window at the front of the building, not the side. Once inside, my friend and I would sneak up the stairs to her fourth-floor apartment.

We did this a few times, until one day, as I walked into the side door, to my horror, I saw the superintendent standing there with her arms crossed, with a repulsed look curling on her face. She probably saw me walking past the front entrance and was able to figure out my side-door plan.

She shook her head. "No. Get out. We already have a roach infestation," she said as she pointed at the door. That was the last time I ever entered that building.

Two Cultures

Asian immigrants are confronted with living between two cultures: the East and the West. This bicultural existence demands that they understand how to navigate multiple social groups, languages, histories, cultures, and religions. Asian Americans often get caught in between multiple cultures and feel unable to measure up to and belong in either. The situation is all the more fraught for Asian American women, who today must traverse the slippery patriarchal standards of traditional Asian culture while navigating the dynamics of eroticization and dominant white feminist culture. While life in between two cultures seems to be the way forward in a globalizing world, this type of life often faces clashing and competing values, understandings, and beliefs.

In my own personal experiences, I often found myself trying to please and appease my parents by maintaining my Korean identity and language at home, while simultaneously trying to lose them whenever I left the house. I felt the need to extinguish my Korean identity because the outside world saw me as a foreigner, and like all children, I had a desire to feel wanted and included. Many of my Korean friends tried dying their hair and dressing like the white kids. Some even put a tiny sliver of clear tape on their eyelids, creating a fold to make their eyes look larger. However, with my awkward English, outdated clothes, and unmistakable Asian appearance, I was nowhere close to looking more western and was easily dismissed by my peers.

Marginal people's self-alienation stems from their external alienation by dominant societies. The self is split in two when marginalized people are torn between two worlds. Sociologist Everett Stonequist states, "The duality of cultures produces a duality of personality—a divided self."[46] The marginal person is then a cultural schizophrenic. The person seems out of touch with reality as their sense of reality is distorted by the dominant white society. The duality of self can be illustrated by two mirrors: when two mirrors reflect a self simultaneously, each shows a different side of the self, which gives rise to a dual self-consciousness. Just as marginality arises out of conflicting worlds, self-alienation results from conflicting selves in a personality.[47] The alienation of the self is difficult to overcome. Alienation from society compounds self-alienation, causing complex and lasting psychological damage.

Being caught in this strange gray area (either-or and neither-nor) is difficult for a child who has barely begun to establish or understand their identity. This in-between existence is a common experience among immigrants: we are *neither* this nor that while also *being* this and that. Immigrants belong fully to neither their native culture nor their host culture. When immigrants travel back to their country of origin, they often recognize that they do not fit in there either. They often feel that their country of origin has changed, becoming more distant and foreign.

In-Betweenness

Jung Young Lee, a Korean American theologian, articulates the marginalization of Asian Americans and their feelings of in-betweenness.[48] Asian Americans are in a liminal state between the homeland and the host land. Asian Americans are cognizant of the fact that while they are immersed in both cultures, they are situated in a perpetual state of uncertainty.

In-betweenness is the sense that Asian Americans belong to both Asia and America, though not fully. They dwell in the intersections between two cultures.[49] This in-betweenness can be harmful psychologically and spiritually. It can lead to an undefined, insecure self-identity—often to a sense of rootlessness and an inordinate desire for belonging.[50] There are consequences and limitations of being in between two cultures, especially if one is rejected by both.

I remember my first trip back to Korea in 1982, seven years after immigration. My relatives said that I spoke "funny" and that I didn't sound Korean at all anymore. They made sure to remind me that I was not the same person who left Korea carrying the red bags. Over that summer, I came to realize that it was not just my family but other Koreans on the street, in parks, and at shopping centers who all looked at me as a foreigner, as I talked differently and even dressed differently from the rest of Korean society. It was unsettling for me to recognize that the people I thought I identified most with did not think I was like them at all. Later, I realized this was true.

In an in-between existence, a marginal person exists between two or more social worlds and suffers from a crisis of identity and lack of self-recognition. In the margins, one is always in a state of conflict. One feels guilt either for opposing one's own culture and surrendering to the dominant, mainstream culture or for distancing oneself from the dominant society in order to remain closer to one's original culture.

Asian Americans' experience of in-betweenness is neither temporary nor voluntary. They are forced to remain in between—that is, not American but an Asian type of American, not an Asian but an American type of Asian. They are alienated not only from their cultural worlds but also from themselves. Asian Americans are pulled toward several identities and deprived of a singular self-image. This marginality is a coerced in-betweenness, or an in-betweenness that is made seemingly permanent by the dominant group.[51] The disorientation Asian Americans experience subordinates them and keeps them in a marginalized state of mind and form.

Socially, to be in between is to be part of a minority, a member of a marginalized group. Culturally, it means not being fully integrated into and accepted by either cultural system. Linguistically, the betwixt-and-between person is bilingual but may not achieve mastery in either language and often speaks with a distinct accent. Psychologically and spiritually, the person does not possess a well-defined and secure self-identity and is often marked by excessive impressionableness, rootlessness, and an inordinate desire for belonging. An Asian American will never be American enough; because of their race and culture, *American* will function only as a qualifier for the noun *Asian*. However, to be betwixt and between is not totally negative and need not cause cultural schizophrenia. Paradoxically, being neither this nor that allows one to be both this and that. An Asian American is American in a way no other American can be.[52]

We must see the power in living in liminal spaces. Liminality comes from the Latin word *limen*, which means "threshold."

A person in a state of transition, or on the threshold, is in a liminal state, a place of limbo, neither here nor there, or in the words of anthropologist Victor Turner, "betwixt and between the positions assigned and arranged by law, culture, convention and ceremonial."[53] Minority groups like Asian Americans can experience liminality. They feel that they are between two places and, as such, are never fully integrated into society. They can be part of their own Asian culture but not part of the white American culture.

A liminal space is one of transition; therefore, it is temporary. To be in a temporary location brings anxiety and uneasiness that can eventually break down one's spirit. However, some are able to use this space in a good way. For them, liminality functions in a positive way to provide an alternative creative space. Being in between means being both invisible and necessary to culture. There is creative potential in recognizing, owning, and accepting one's liminal space in contrast to white/male dominance and Asian/female passivity. Liminal spaces that are inhabited by Asian Americans are places of innovation and progress.

Liminality provides a space where an alternative reality can be enacted—namely, in the form of *communitas*. *Communitas* is a Latin word that describes an unstructured community of equality and signifies a strong spirit of community. *Communitas* challenges society to rethink and reform its way of doing things by proposing new paradigms and models that invert or subvert the old. Liminality functions in a positive and transformative way when these new and subversive models are incorporated into the existing structure and center of society. Liminality's creative potential consists of its capacity (1) to bring about an openness to the new and the possible and (2) to challenge and transform the existing society by offering prophetic and subversive knowledge and criticism and envisioning and enacting new ideas and models.

Redefining Korean American Women

History, religion, and culture define women, and most of these defining aspects are influenced by men. Stories told by women have the power to change the social discourse, transform culture, and reinvent women's sense of self. Women, especially Korean American women, must be emboldened to cultivate, craft, and share their stories in order to change the hypersexualized narrative that has been imposed on them. By writing their own stories, women take back power. Once the narrative changes, new ideas about Korean American women in culture and society can emerge.

Korean American women need to resist the reappropriation of cultural terms and artifacts. They must find the agency to create a new lexicon by which they define themselves, particularly to move away from the dangerous perceptions of Asian women as hypersexualized beings and move toward individual empowerment. This change in language will help dictate the way in which women describe and thus understand themselves. In this process, Korean American women will be encouraged to imagine, to speak imaginatively, and to demand space for themselves as leaders.

Korean American women have traditionally been praised for their quietness as they lived out the old dictum "Women should be seen and not heard." Silence was viewed as a virtuous characteristic of women. Furthermore, women must recognize that knowledge is power.[54] Thus, women need to acquire knowledge to balance the scales. Korean American women must study their history, culture, and religion so that their knowledge can help propel them to a better future. Understanding why oppression exists will help bring about its elimination. Specifically, understanding how racism and sexism emerge and manifest in the church is a helpful step toward eliminating them from the church.

The interdisciplinary theological field of Korean American women is neither monolithic nor homogeneous. Rather, it is hybrid and complex, present in multiple categories. As a result, Korean American women's theology needs to take its own in-between context, heritage, and categories into consideration to develop a hybrid spirituality that addresses the specific concerns of Korean American women. Feminist theology emerged to address white women's experiences; Korean American women's experiences, however, are drastically different. Korean Americans' church lives are also drastically different, as Korean culture and heritage are influential in worship, governance, and church life. Therefore, both theology and church are contextual. The context for Korean American theology includes the historical immigration story and the ongoing US neocolonialism and militarism that impacts Koreans and Korean Americans.

We must take gender seriously as an analytic category. It has been used to look at the ways identities, experiences, and relationships are built. It also provides a lens to examine theological notions, assumptions, and agendas that have been considered "universal."[55] But as this chapter has illustrated, gender is viewed and experienced in different ways depending on the context and culture. We must work toward justice by examining and identifying the ways in which gender has been used by religion and culture to oppress women.

Conclusion

The long, tumultuous history of Asian American immigration, marked with racial bans and discriminatory practices, lends itself to an Asian America that is fraught with insecurity and profound ambition. For many Asian Americans, their consciousness of being Asian triggers a meteoric urge to run from their history, their buried cultural identities—to run far ahead of the rest of society without looking back. Many do this because they believe it is how they will become visible in a society that continually refuses to see them and makes no room for their presence—not in fearful animosity but in pale ambivalence.

When Asians first arrived as indentured laborers, making just enough money to send back home to support their families, they worked under harsh conditions for low wages. The fear of Asians, the Chinese in particular, inspired laws such as the 1882 Chinese Exclusion Act, which was designed to stop the Chinese from entering and gaining citizenship. Yellow Peril was woven into the laws, culture, and attitudes of white American society. Yet even though some Asian immigrants have achieved monumental success, made radical accomplishments, and acquired a mass of new wealth, they continue to be invisible.

As Asian immigrants tried to cope with the difficulties they encountered in their new country, they came to recognize their own in-betweenness. Asian Americans live in two cultures but belong to neither; as such, many struggle to survive and thrive in the United States. However, this liminal space has been a subversive, creative and radical space for many Asian immigrants like me. With all of its hardships and struggles, liminality has shaped and molded us into who we are. For some of us, it has given us strength and resilience to try to cultivate new lives in a new land. As we build a new voice for ourselves as individuals and as a greater community, we embrace our differences to cultivate strength.

3

RACISM
Yellow People

Racial discussions in America are largely shaped by polarizing black-and-white racial dialogues. The category *Asian American* was not even recognized and named until the late 1960s, despite Asians inhabiting North America for several centuries prior.[1] Those who adopted the term did so in an effort to consolidate the political forces of various immigrant communities. *Asian American* as a category traverses ethnic borders and class divisions, spanning from Southeast Asian refugees who struggle to adapt to white American society, to families spanning generations of American residency who hold only an abstract relationship to their ancestral origins and to children of elite Chinese transnationals sent to the United States for education, among others. While the perception of Asian Americans today has ties to East Asians—namely, Chinese, Japanese, Taiwanese, and Koreans—who are believed to be some of the most educated and economically prosperous groups in the country, the term *Asian American* encompasses the most economically divided ethnic and racial group in the United States.[2] Within this disparity, perhaps what unifies Asian America through history and present life is a poignant sense of otherness and the dismissal of the experience Asian Americans share and the cultural spaces they occupy.

Racism against Asian Americans is seldom recognized. Terms such as *perpetual foreigners*, *honorary whites*, and *model minority* have been used to minimize their plight, rendering their experiences peripheral, invisible, and nonexistent. Xenophobia contributes to the rise of racism and discrimination toward Asian Americans, as they are constantly viewed within binaries that work to either attack their viability as "true" Americans or falsely elevate their personal abilities to pit them against other racialized minorities. Xenophobia, on the one hand, does not welcome Asian Americans as true Americans; on the other hand, it promotes Asian Americans above other marginalized groups.

This distorted elevation of Asian competency is a tool used by white society to polarize minority populations. Asian American elevation has led to the degradation of brown, Black, Latinx, and Indigenous peoples, creating tension among these communities. This scheme has also worked to invalidate, trivialize, or at times, scorn the issues that Asian Americans face. This also allows for the dismissal of all the complex contributions Asian Americans make. They are neither worthy of dignified recognition nor valued for their individual output as they confront a distinct cultural landscape.

Asian Americans carefully tread through the barriers between white America, Asian America, and their motherland, all of which encompass varied expectations. These diverse expectations especially affect Asian American women, as they sit at the intersection of marginalization—facing subjugation from a conservative, patriarchal ethnic community and discrimination from the prevailing Western culture. These forces of marginalization take a toll on Asian American women's wellness and well-being. Additionally, in religious spaces, Asian American women have long been subject to religious and cultural patriarchy that contribute to their lack of visibility in society and the church.

What Are You?

When I arrived in Canada at the age of five, I spoke no English. Not being able to communicate with this new world gave me enough reason to turn away from it altogether. I retreated into myself, barely speaking and barely interacting with this new world that was yet to be deciphered.

My withdrawal became even more evident during recess at school. When break time came around, I became increasingly anxious, short of breath, and hot around my ears. Classmates burst through the door at the bell, but I would slink out, always late, ready to hear the goading chants, "Ching-chong, ching-chong!" I am not sure how it came to be, but for those first few years of school, I was referred to as "the quiet Chink" or "the Jap." I felt not only undeserving of a real name but undeserving of sympathy from those at the school who should have sought to protect me. I remember kids striding toward me, asking me why I smelled, why I didn't talk, and why my eyes looked that way. I remember one particular classmate pushing his hand up to my face and asking me if I could even see it.

Teachers would ask me, "Where are you from?" while classmates would challenge me with the "*What* are you?" question. I always replied, "I am Korean." But I was frequently told that there was no such thing. Some children seemed to think *Korean* was an amalgamation of Chinese and Japanese. Confused and taken aback, I routinely went home crying, asking my mother time and time again if there was such a thing as Korea and if Koreans were truly real. My mom assured me that there was in fact such a country, recalling our old house, our family, our little dog, our birds, and our garden—they were in Korea, they were Korean. But I could not bear to think about all we had left behind—it was too fresh of a loss. Thus I became numb, indignant, and then defiant at the motherland, the heritage and the home that were seemingly taken from me.

Xenophobia

When we ask "*What* are you?" rather than "*Who* are you?" we bring into question what defines American identity, but perhaps more specifically, we bring into question what defines *racial* American identity. The country's founding documents outline the basic rights to be bestowed on Americans: equality; the fundamental rights to life, liberty, and the pursuit of happiness; and the right of the people to govern themselves democratically. But who actually is acknowledged as an American through the eyes of fellow Americans is not always clear.

The designation of the title *American* is deeply influenced by the xenophobia, racism, and discrimination that course through the American story, from the country's founding to its contemporary view of itself. Xenophobia has been part of America's immigration tradition, determining who can or cannot enter our so-called nation of immigrants. Even as Americans have realized that the threats allegedly posed by immigrants are unjustified, they have allowed xenophobic behavior to move from de facto practice to institutional law.

The Greek word *xenos* means "stranger" or "foreign," and *phobos* means "fear" or "flight." *Xenophobia* quite literally means "fear and hatred of foreigners," and it manifests as individual and institutional prejudice and bias against foreigners. It promotes an irrational fear and hatred of immigrants that often results in the demonization of the foreigner (and those considered to be foreign). When the Chinese came to the United States as indentured workers, many were afraid of them, which eventually led to the Chinese Exclusion Act of 1882. There was much anti-Chinese sentiment, or Sinophobia. During the COVID-19 pandemic, with the rise of anti-Asian racism, the fear of Chinese or all Asians was rampant.

When fear drives xenophobia, as it has most recently in the pandemic, it loads negative associations onto targeted groups. Immigrants have been equated to economic threats that demand federal attention to limit the immigration of people of color.[3] Xenophobia stems from a narrow definition of who is American and who is not. It exists and flourishes during times of peace and war, economic prosperity and depression, low and high immigration, and racial struggle and racial progress. It has shaped all aspects of American life, influencing policy and shifting America's definitions of race, citizenship, and what it means to be American—all of which has sustained white supremacy and rising nationalism.[4]

White America precisely defines who and what is American, which denotes privileged selectivity in choosing who can immigrate and become naturalized according to what they feel is acceptable. When the Chinese Exclusion Act expired, it was extended by the Geary Act of 1892, which barred the Chinese from entering the United States. The Geary Act ended in 1943. There was also the Immigration Act of 1917, also known as the Asiatic Barred Zone Act, which stopped immigration from any country adjacent to Asia.[5] During World War II, Japanese Americans lost everything they possessed and were forced into internment camps as they became national threats to white Americans.

Race and the American cultural perception of one's race have been the determining factors in distinguishing between the "good" immigrants and the "bad" ones, the better assimilable ones from the unassimilable ones, the racialized ones and the neutral ones.[6] Immigrants deemed worthy of American citizenship were naturalized; those who were not were excluded. The McCarran-Walter Act (1952) abolished the racial restrictions put in place by the Naturalization Act of 1790, which limited naturalization to "free white persons." This meant women, nonwhite persons, and indentured servants (who were mostly Asian Americans) could not become naturalized citizens. Over time, access to citizenship became more expansive, but the racial restriction was not eliminated entirely until 1952. This produced the category of "aliens" who were ineligible for citizenship, which largely affected Asian immigrants and limited their rights as noncitizens to property ownership, representation in courts, public employment, and voting.[7] Thus many generations of Asian Americans were made invisible. Without citizenship, they were pushed to the margins, and they did not have the rights to challenge their marginality and invisibility in the courts.

Xenophobia is a defining feature of American life. Xenophobia emerged as soon as nonwhites immigrated to America and triumphed in the 1920s. The 1924 Johnson-Reed Act was a strict policy of ethnic quotas that nearly closed the door on immigration from Asia for over forty years. When mainstream, explicit forms of xenophobia began to wane during the civil rights movement, it merely bubbled away from the surface, still lurking, only to reemerge in the last half century—namely, during the Trump administration.[8]

Xenophobia has continued the legacy of discriminatory immigration policies, such as the Muslim ban (2017) introduced by President Trump, banning foreigners from seven predominantly Muslim countries from visiting the United States for ninety days. Xenophobia continues to marginalize immigrants and people of color who have been in America for centuries. For example, many employers may not hire potential employees if they bear an "ethnic name" for fear that they may not be American enough for the role. This common employment discrimination has led many people of color to anglicize or change their names to sound "American."[9] Thus nonanglicized names of Asian Americans will make them appear foreign even though they have been living in the United States for generations.

Xenophobia has also driven nativism, the naming of white Anglo-Saxon Protestant settlers and their descendants as native to the United States, ignoring the Indigenous populations. This designation led to granting special privileges and protections to them, which prompted antiforeign sentiment. White Protestants believed they should be recognized as "true" Americans. A deep-rooted fear of displacement drove these early and enduring expressions of nativism and white supremacy.[10] It has allowed for the malicious superiority that has built systems of abuse, most notably a criminal justice system that disproportionately targets and incarcerates Black and brown men. White nativism feeds into white supremacy, instilling hatred and fear toward other races. White supremacy continues to put a wedge between people of color and white people, cultivating conflict within communities that fuels discrimination. Unfortunately, this discrimination is seldom discussed outside of black-and-white dialogues, polarities that ignore the racism that is experienced by other communities of color.

Generations of anti-immigrant leaders, politicians, and citizens have adapted xenophobic ideologies to identify perceived threats and enact new solutions to the "problem" of immigration.[11] Xenophobia has become normalized through successful repetition, expanding on an established anti-immigrant playbook to sway public opinion and policy against immigration. During and after the successful exclusion of Chinese immigrants, groups considered to be similar to the Chinese—such as Japanese, Koreans, South Asians, and Filipinos—were similarly condemned to immigration restriction and exclusion. The exclusion of Asian immigrants in the past seeps into current rhetoric and policy. Equality between whites and people of color must continue to be fought for.

Despite their long history in the United States, Asian Americans, particularly women, have been seen as foreigners who are unable to fully assimilate into the dominant culture. This nonacceptance is mainly due to the appearance of Asian Americans as non-American-looking—in other words, nonwhite. Nonwhiteness has been a major factor in preventing Asian Americans from obtaining full inclusion within American society.

Race and Its History

From the seventeenth century, American white supremacists (imported from the English, Spanish, French, and Dutch) viewed race as biologically determined rather than socially constructed. Race was based on skin color differences. Asians were labeled *yellow* in the nineteenth century by the West. The color yellow was a racial marker that had been imbued with new meaning in relation to the white norm. Whites were at the top and Blacks were at the bottom of a fabricated, yet enforced, racial hierarchy.[12]

Historical racial divides (that continue into the present) increase gender divides in American immigrant communities and become a deconstructing force within the communal body. Oppressed people tend to oppress others who have less power than themselves, and in patriarchal Asian American communities, men have power over women. As Asian American men experience racism in society, their internalized anger, marginalization, oppression, and fear are played out in the home as they turn to oppressing their wives within the private domain of their homes and within Asian American immigrant communities such as the church. Asian American men's contributions to the oppression of Asian American women today are made clear through the women's conflicted existence within and outside their racial/ethnic communities. This is evident in the latent divides between Asian American women and men, who culturally subordinate women, and between Asian American women and white American women, who indirectly make Asian American women's marginalization invisible through their own dominance in Western feminist dialogues. In conjunction, white American women contribute to the erasure of Asian American women's contributions and presence in American society.

Racism

Racism is a tool that has been used by a dominant white society to maintain its status and cultural influence. When consciously used to oppress people of color, racism favors the dominant group and keeps the subordinate group in their lower status. Racism pushes Asian Americans into the margins in order to maintain white Americans' status and place in society.

Covert racism, often appearing as microaggressions, can be subconscious, nondeliberate, and rarely recognized by the perpetrators—or even the victims themselves.[13] Microaggressions are common verbal and behavioral actions that are subtle but hostile and derogatory. They often occur when negative stereotypes are justified by the model minority myth, which masks blatant discrimination against Asian Americans with their supposed prosperity.

Racism promotes the exclusion of vulnerable and powerless members of society from basic social equality and opportunity by classes who believe they are the only ones fully entitled to the benefits of economic, social, cultural, and intellectual spheres.[14] Through racism, privileged groups dominate smaller or more vulnerable groups based on the idea that dominant beliefs, values, and cultural practices are the norm, making all other cultures and social practices subject to judgment, objectification, and marginalization. Racism has been woven into the American culture; as such, it perpetuates the values of those who feel a sense of entitlement.[15]

Racism has become internalized by those who believe there is a center in society that can be maintained through the survival of the status quo and the continuation of racial hierarchies. Asian Americans can be consumed by their marginal status, which often results in the perpetuation of their oppression, as they believe that their marginality is inherent or rationalized. Stereotypes about weakness, low self-esteem, and strong appearance biases that are communicated socioculturally are effectively interiorized by a large portion of Asian Americans. This could be in part due to Asian Americans' propensity toward cultural homogeneity and communal harmony, which may foster a more unified racial identity and racial self-image.[16]

Perpetual Foreigners

Despite discriminatory laws being struck down and social attitudes shifting toward displays of diversity and inclusivity, Asian Americans are still weakened in their social and political presence. Presently, Asian Americans occupy a unique space on the fringes of Black and white, foreign and American, privilege and poverty. Depending on the current state of affairs, certain immigrant groups tend to be labeled by the dominant culture as good or bad, agreeable or problematic. Asian American groups have most often been categorized as good, agreeable immigrants, a status that is upheld by the myths of the model minority and the honorary white.

However, Asian Americans can also be perceived negatively as perpetual foreigners, religious others, and unassimilated refugees. These labels and stereotypes serve myriad purposes. During the Cold War, the Asian American model minority who achieved the American dream was held up as proof of American exceptionalism and meritocracy at a time when the United States was being criticized by communist rivals abroad and civil rights activists at home. The model minority myth was used to perpetuate the notion that all it takes to achieve the American dream is the will to work hard enough, signifying the idealism of American meritocracy under the guise of Asian American diligence.

The model minority myth gained even more traction in American public discourse during the 1980s, when newspapers and magazines routinely praised Asian Americans for holding the formula for success.[17] This praise was both similar to and different from the attention Asian Americans have received in previous decades. Like the 1960s version of the Asian American model minority stereotype, the 1980s edition also explained Asian American success through so-called Asian values that emphasized a traditional reverence for learning and strong family structures. This description distances Asians from other Americans, as "Asian values" reputably focus on filial piety and loyalty to family, corporation, and nation rather than individualism.[18]

The perceived educational and socioeconomic successes of Asian Americans are used to compare them to other racial minorities. This strategy only benefits whites, pitting Asian Americans against African Americans, Latinxs, and other racial minority groups to relieve white Americans of their responsibility for their privilege and contribution to socioeconomic racial divides. It essentially allows whites to say that if you just work hard enough, study hard enough, read enough, and so on, you can and should succeed like Asian Americans.

But this is a myth perpetuated by white supremacy to maintain the status quo and cause racialized minorities to fight among themselves. Undoubtedly, not all Asian Americans are successful, attend elite schools, are able to have a high income, and live in desirable neighborhoods. Just a quick visit to Queens, New York, will reveal a community of working class Asian Americans living in poverty. There you will find a large community of Asian Americans living with their extended families in small units with shared kitchens and bathrooms and bedrooms. It goes without saying, not all Asian Americans are successful, prosperous, and living the American dream.

On the one hand, white Americans use the model minority myth to describe Asian Americans; on the other hand, they treat them as perpetual foreigners. Many Asian Americans who have been in America for five or six generations are still asked "Where are you from?"—that is, "What country are you from?"—inferring their supposed foreignness and otherness. This reveals how Asian Americans cannot be "real" or "natural" Americans but will continue to be viewed as foreigners.

White Americans' portrayal of Asian Americans as foreigners has also created the precarious position of the "probationary American," or someone who is still being tested and observed in order to claim their American identity. This is in sharp contrast to the model minority myth, in which Asian Americans are elevated and superficially revered as being idealized people of color. This dichotomy between the positive and negative stereotypes is part of the reason why Asian Americans possess such a confused sense of racial and cultural identity. Often, they are used as pawns by white Americans to benefit the dominant and elite class. If Asian Americans are viewed as an influx of probationary immigrants, they are subject to a trial period that has no time limit in order to prove themselves as "true Americans"—a status they can never obtain because of their distinctly racialized appearance.

As foreigners, Asian Americans are perceived as existing exterior to the main body of American culture and society, held far outside the perimeters of white physiognomy and culture. The persistence in treating Asian Americans as outsiders in their own country has resulted in everyday racial slights, microaggressions, and internalized racism as well as targeted violence and hate crimes. Asian Americans must put themselves into more race-related discussions, as they are important in understanding the ways in which race operates today.[19] Asian Americans' experiences of racial discrimination should not be made invisible due to their minority myth status or their portrayal as perpetual foreigners. Asian Americans are just as American as white Americans.

During the 2016 presidential election, *New York Times* writer Michael Lou recounted what happened to him after church when a white woman confronted him in the streets of Lower Manhattan. He was born in the United States but is of Chinese ancestry, and while he was walking with his young daughter, a white woman yelled at him and told him to "go back home,"[20] a phrase often said angrily to Asian Americans. To this white woman, Michael Lou was a foreigner and could not possibly be perceived as an American. According to her, he needed to go back to Asia, his supposed "real" home. Surely, many Asian Americans have heard this kind of rhetoric at some point in their lives.

Asians are constantly questioned regarding their native status and their communicative competency. A few years back, I went into the emergency room after I collapsed in church. While in the ER, every nurse, doctor, and hospital worker who came into my room asked me first, "Do you speak English?" After being admitted to the hospital, I was continually asked the same question over the course of four days by everyone who treated me. The assumed linguistic discord between Asians and Europeans further prevents dominant society from viewing Asians as "American."

The racial distancing upheld by whites against Asians reached a uniquely public, widespread anxiety that was long dormant in the supposed "wokeness" of the current cultural climate. Coming through in painful reprise, racist attacks, both verbal and physical, against Asian Americans surged during the 2020–21 coronavirus pandemic. Historically, pandemics have often heightened discrimination against minorities.[21] These stressful times tend to bring an intensified fear of the other and worsened racist misconceptions about foreigners being either diseased or unclean. For instance, in 1858, a mob burned down a large quarantined hospital on Staten Island as local fear of Irish immigrants thought to be carrying yellow fever came to a head. The distinction between fear and vigilance becomes hazy. Vigilance is crucial in protecting the population as a whole; however, latent societal prejudices can become intensified when people are inclined to distrust one another.

This general distrust only worsened with former President Donald Trump continually referring to COVID-19 as the "Chinese virus." Hate crimes rose and anxiety grew into increasing hostility. "Go back home" quickly turned into something far more sinister. Thirty percent of Americans witnessed someone blaming Asian people for the coronavirus pandemic.[22] This discrimination could not have been facilitated if the perpetual foreigner perception had not been upheld. If Asian Americans were indeed truly viewed, understood, and valued as fully Americans, they would not have been condemned purely by racial association. When Italy became the worse affected country in the world, there was absolutely no anxiety around Italian American immigrants, as their perceived danger—their infectiousness—was only limited to Italians residing in Italy. Unlike Europeans, Asians do not have the same experience of immediate approval by American society. Asians have never been fully welcomed in America and it is crucial to understand the temporary status of the first Asians who came to America shaped the legacy of racism today.

Today, Asian Americans are pushed into an ambiguous space wherein their supposed political meekness and social reserve prohibit others from viewing them as cultural leaders. They are not represented in positions of power or seen making visible change, in part because American society does not believe in them doing so. This can be attributed to the model minority myth—white society believes Asian Americans have already achieved success, so these immigrants do not need support for further mobility. Thus, through ambitious activism and diverse dialogues, Asian Americans must redefine their cultural past, which has rendered their discrimination invisible and unimportant in the American story. In this racially ambiguous space and probationary national identity, Asian Americans have remained silent and apathetically endured small injustices as part of their daily existence.

In recent decades, American culture has shifted from being fearfully hateful of Asians to lauding them, proclaiming the "rise of Asian Americans" to be the exemplar for all other immigrants and ethnic minorities. They are not only the fastest-growing group in the United States but supposedly the most educated and wealthy. This is in stark contrast to the 1800s and the beginning of the 1900s, when discrimination, racism, and xenophobia marked Asian immigrants as undesirable and un-American.

Researchers at the Pew Research Center have declared that Asian American achievement as a whole represents major milestones of economic success and social assimilation in the United States. Even as they acknowledge differences among Asian Americans, the Pew researchers found that as a group, they enjoyed shared economic mobility, high education rates, and collectively valued "cultural" traits such as the importance of family, respect for elders, and a "pervasive belief in the rewards of hard work."[23] While these traits have been generally attributed as positive by the dominant culture, they have also become sweeping oversimplifications that minimize the struggles of Asian Americans. For instance, the Asian American demographic actually has the largest gap in income equality; the poorest in this group fare worse economically compared to all racial groups. Because this gap is rarely discussed, the "typical" Asian American is depicted as an East Asian, highly educated, middle-upper-class citizen. Statistics show that 1.1 million Southeast Asian Americans are low income, and 460,000 live in poverty.[24] The skewed statistics push a public misperception that contributes to the perceived privilege Asian Americans have over all other ethnic minorities and even the dominant white American class. In truth, Asian America encompasses one of the most heterogeneous, complex, innovative, and changing demographics in the country, ranging from multigenerational Asian American families, to Hmong and Vietnamese refugees escaping political violence and poverty, to wealthy young generation of international students from Taiwan, Singapore, and China.

Once cast as racially inferior foreigners who threatened national welfare and "real" American culture, Asian Americans are now the poster child of success in the country, even going so far as being titled "honorary whites." But this portrait is deceitful. It eliminates inequalities and disparities among Asian Americans and relies on a new and divisive language of racism; the title obscures the unstable place of Asian Americans in contemporary America, falsely elevating them so they are not able to have real issues addressed due to their assumed advantage. Depending on domestic economic and global political conditions, some Asian Americans are accepted as full and equal citizens in the United States, while others find themselves marginalized as dangerous outsiders.[25]

Invisibility

Asian Americans, like most other immigrants and ethnic minorities, must be able to walk in at least two different worlds with two different cultural systems. They must be able to maneuver through the intricacies of racism, xenophobia, discrimination, and marginality to survive in the new world they ultimately must forge for themselves. While these two worlds, white America and Asian America, possess complex structures of power, it is often the case that one of them prevents an individual from attaining the same level of power as they do in the other. The one that withholds the power is white America due to its systemic racism, discrimination, and xenophobia.

In my experiences of racism, I remember wishing for a particular superpower. I grew up watching the television show *Invisible*

Man, whose titular character was able to make himself invisible. I envied him. If my physical being, my speech, my clothes, or my scent could have left no trace, it would have been so much easier to go on living peacefully, without anyone's judgments shaping my reality and even how I thought about myself.

It is one thing to make oneself invisible; it is another to become invisible without choice. Becoming invisible through no choice of my own, I realize the damaging power that racism has on minoritized individuals and communities. I become invisible when society does not value me or my concerns. Society ignores the plight of Asian Americans and dismisses their struggles by using terms such as *honorary whites* and *model minority*. When I tell colleagues or people at church about my experiences of racism, they usually tell me, "That is not racism," as Asians are almost white and don't experience racism. Ignoring my suffering from discrimination and marginalization is making me invisible and pushing me aside. When Asian Americans internalize that erasure and begin to behave within the confines of this construct, the long reach of white supremacy is revealed. Invisibility is not just created and maintained by dominant groups but internalized and upheld by the marginalized.

White American power over Asian Americans is created through cultural, social, and religious practices that are revalidated and reinforced until the oppressive practices undermine and obscure the Asian American. These practices may become so commonplace that the oppression is normalized and indiscernible to both the oppressor and the oppressed. In the normalization of Asian invisibility, we grapple with the loss of communal agency, a major detriment to day-to-day work and life caused by damaging power imbalances. Both parties are harmed in this process, but for the oppressed, their powerlessness drains the mind and soul.

When Asian Americans are made invisible, it is done to justify someone else's sense of superiority. White America's position of primacy is defined and shaped by the oppression of others and the eradication of their agency. Without equal opportunity and agency, Asian Americans become imperceptible in society. Becoming unnoticeable leads us down a well-traveled route that many have taken in pursuit of integrating into America. Yet in a relatively young country founded on migration and immigration, foreign identities and invisibility converge in the fabric of racial diversity where racial hierarchies are created to establish dominance amid variance. This relationship between visibility and foreignness is part of the reason it has always been so difficult to accept Asian Americans as American. This begs the question: Who gets to be an American?

Asian Americans and Marginality

Marginality is understood as a place where tensions occur between groups of people of varying races and cultures.[26] Minority peoples who are visibly different tend to be categorized as "other" and are pushed to alternative spaces in society that are at various points of distance from the center. Second- or third-generation Asian Americans are often easily acculturated and adopted into the American lifestyle, but they cannot be fully assimilated into American society because of their race and ethnicity. Thus one of the most basic markers of marginality is one's race.[27]

Because of their continued oppression, marginalized people can become hypersensitive about their racial origins. In consequence, many—Asian Americans specifically—can acquire an inferiority complex. Other psychological symptoms include ambivalence, excessive self-consciousness, restlessness, lack of self-confidence, pessimism, and sentimentalism. The dominant social norm defines the margin, and thus negative traits in a minority group are emphasized in the broad culture and affect personality formation in the minority. Such minority traits may be accurate for the dominant group but are incorrect for the minority depicted. The characteristics of the marginalized are seen as negative and inferior. However, the marginalized have the potential to be acute and able critics of the dominant group and its culture. The spaces in between boundaries create a marginal condition. Marginality is more than a boundary itself; it has a width where two or more cultures intermix. People from different cultures may be brought together as well as separated. The place where new ideas encounter a culture is this "in-between" place, a nexus where two or more worlds interconnect. Boundaries and meeting places present conditions that offer opportunities for creativity. The idea of interconnectedness leads us to an awareness of being in both worlds. This self-affirming definition balances the self-negating understanding of the dominant group as seen by a marginal group(s).[28]

Asian Americans are marginalized people who live between two cultures. Being in-between means belonging to neither fully. They are alienated not only from the dominant worlds but from themselves, a condition that deprives them of an integrated self-image. The norm of marginality moves from the center to the boundary between the margins; the norm is from the outside to the inside, the other to the self. This movement and change in defining marginality are historically inevitable.[29]

In a pluralistic society, the norm for those existing "beyond the fringe" is planted, fertilized, and nurtured in the boundary between cultures. Asian Americans seek identities, claim their rightful places, and stand as one of many ethnicities in the new social, political, and cultural configuration of North America.[30] Asian Americans affirm their identity and their right to be equal, but their equality is not entirely achieved.

Marginality puts one at the border between two worlds but also denotes that one may lose their independent place. Transcendence for newer cultural communities is possible only by joining hands in the space between the marginal and central cultures. The margin occurs because of two or more centers of culture. However, people can build creative centers in the margins, which can result in the larger movement of innovation in the expanding center. This creative nexus does not replace the older center but becomes a new connection in a new place where cultures meet.[31]

Asian Americans must be cognizant of how their acclimation to central perspectives and central thinking distorts the experience of those in the margins. As the margins expand and contract, the center often remains the same, encompassing all significant action. The margin, malleable and reactive to its environment, is receptive to the changing dynamics at the center. As a result, those in the center can enforce changes to the detriment of those in the margin. Thus, those in the margins and those in the center must find a way to create a balance between them. This means exalting the marginalized and celebrating the oppressed to reach harmony; in doing so, we can find a new, authentic center that liberates rather than subjugates.

Margins can be a place of creativity, and new centers can be formed in the margins; likewise, margins can be formed in the center.[32] These two categories are not static but rather fluid and dynamic. An immovable center is a false idea, and a return to this concept can resurrect dangerous ideas that were once central to western society. A person might consider themselves as being at the margin, while others could perceive that individual as being situated at the center—for example, Asian American leaders who are marginalized in the larger American society but are influential in the center of Asian American communities. It is hard to differentiate between centrality and marginality, as they are dependent on the subject's and the object's perspectives and are comparative to the contexts in which we define our rank. It is important to understand the relativity of multiple centers and margins when we study the marginality of ethnic minorities.[33]

Despite all their contributions to American life, Asian Americans still exist in the margins, relegated as background characters and mere landscape to dominant society. The invisibility of Asian Americans in American history is painful, and we must continue to remember the indentured workers' history, the lack of voting rights until 1943, the Japanese internment, and Asian Americans' experience of being "perpetual foreigners" in a country they have lived in for hundreds of years. The systemic racism against Asian immigrants has too often been ignored or dismissed. These injustices continue to marginalize Asian Americans and make them invisible in the dominant white society.

Identity as the Other

European settlers seized Indigenous land and committed genocide against Indigenous peoples. Around the same period, captured and enslaved Africans were brought to the country as the first "others," forging the xenophobic, white supremacy legacy that captured Indigenous land and resources, causing the lasting tyranny against Indigenous peoples and denying basic human rights of the enslaved. Immigrants have fit into this racial environment of settlers, slaves, and Indigenous peoples, retargeting Americans' tendencies toward othering them.[34] Describing certain groups as *savages* and *exotics* is a way to reinforce xenophobia while conveying the message that people of color are racially inferior. It is in the colonial margin that Western culture reveals its difference, its boundary conditions. It is the evasiveness of ambivalence that gives the colonial stereotype its currency and ensures its ability to adapt to changing times and events.[35]

This process of othering happens so frequently to Asian Americans (and we must not forget, within the Asian American community) that we oftentimes fail to resist. We sacrifice our own stories to the colonizers and oppressors, allowing them to retell them as their own and relieve themselves of the animosity and guilt embedded in their histories. The oppressors disguise themselves as liberators of those they have marginalized, claiming that they have now conceded their power to the marginalized—from mere performative remembrance to actuality.[36] Such pretenses must stop; the united marginalized community must find ways to share their own stories with the world—or at least to one another.

Homi K. Bhabha, a postcolonial scholar, writes, "The 'destiny of non-satisfaction' is fulfilled in the recognition of otherness as a symbol (not sign) of the presence of *significance* or *difference*: otherness is the point of equivalence or identity in a circle in which what needs to be proved is assumed."[37] The understanding of otherness becomes fixed in the Western world.

In the space of resistance, we need to reexamine our dialogue and our speech and recognize that some forces and power will silence us. These forces are different from the powers that say, as author bell hooks writes, "Speak, tell me your story, only do not speak with the voice of resistance. Only speak from that space in the margin that is a sign of deprivation, a sign of the wounded, and a sign of unfulfilled longing. Only speak about your pain."[38] The pain causes weakness in our spirit, which we must overcome, and thus we approach the colonizer at the center from a position of spiritual equality.

Hooks was able to resist becoming the other because she recognized that the margin does not have to be a place of domination but rather can be a place of strength and resistance.[39] In that space, that lived-in segregated world of past and present, she was not other. She resisted the push that sought to marginalize her and her work as alternative or tangential and was ultimately met in the center.[40] Hooks shows us how we can resist domination and work toward some form of liberation from oppression.

The Racialization of Asian American Women

When I began teaching, I thought all the faculty were operating under the same rules and on the same field. As much as I wanted to believe it, this was not the case. The stakeholders in white supremacy (though they likely don't realize their own role in it) had created a system in which outsiders—ethnic minorities and women—had to continually contextualize their perspective, their work, and their style under a white heteronormative framework. The unspoken (but sometimes blatantly spoken) principle is that if minorities do not abide by the majority's rules, there will be unpleasant consequences. These consequences most commonly come in the form of further exclusion. Whenever I brought my children into my office, nobody welcomed them, whereas when my male colleagues brought their children in, everyone commented about how they were great fathers with beautiful children, clearly impressed with the very idea of present fatherhood. As years passed, the fact that I brought my child into the office was used against me when it came to evaluations and promotions. It was believed that I was not dedicating enough time to teaching, as I was a mother to three young children, a criticism never presented to any of my male colleagues with families. I know this to be the case with many other female colleagues who are also mothers.

Racialization is a process by which skin color and cultural practices are made out to be socially important markers of difference.[41] Racialized identities are, in part, the result of how the dominant group stereotypes minority groups. On the color scale, whiteness is the ideal, the highest value. Colorism is deeply entrenched in just about every world culture and manifests in beauty standards and skin-lightening practices all across East Asian, Indian, African, and Latinx communities, targeting women who believe that they will be more beautiful, successful, and desirable if their skin is fairer.

To understand Asian American women and the nature of their experience, it is important to understand the context in which they arrived in the United States. Asian women were allowed to immigrate to Hawaii largely because it was an American colony, with only a small percentage of whites and a mostly male population. Asian American women worked in harsh conditions laboring in the sugar plantations or cooking and cleaning for large groups of men living in boarding homes. They experienced both physical and psychological hardship. Initially, Asian American women were viewed as sexual beings in service to men. These perceptions added to the multiple layers of oppression that Asian American women already experienced, often making the conduct toward them demeaning and suggestive. These burdensome labels were and still are odious for Asian American women.

At times, some women wanted to return to Asia, but the high cost of travel generally prevented such movement. This was the case for my mother and me. Seeking to be free of the social limitations and economic constraints in her native country, my mother came to North America only to encounter a different kind of limitation: she was suddenly an outsider and a tertiary character in society. The freedom and liberty she sought in North America had to be quietly, incessantly fought for over time, becoming a pursuit that weaved itself into the fabric of her racial identity.

Asian American women are caught between cultures and influenced by forces beyond their control. In many ways, they have become a colonized people who mimic their colonizers. Iterations of westernization in Asian American life manifest in various ways. Western dominance can encourage people to downplay or hide their cultural beliefs. This phenomenon is commonly observed among subaltern peoples who disguise their own identity behind the mask the colonizer expects to see or imposes.[42] For example, they may minimize their background through language, behavior, and most notably, appearance. As a demographic, Asian women are some of the highest spenders in terms of cosmetic surgery. In hopes of altering their physical appearance, many Asian women make changes to their features to reflect Western facial characteristics more closely. The women submit, mostly unconsciously, to the power of Western beauty ideals and hegemony through plastic surgery and aesthetic maintenance.

In my own experience as a young Korean girl, the unique pressures from within the Korean community to cultivate beauty, to ensure that I was a woman who was valuable, were immeasurable. Korean girls around me would frequently talk about how much they hated their small eyes, flat noses, round faces, and small breasts, wishing that they would one day have plastic surgery to "become pretty." Stuck on many of their eyelids was a thin, clear tape, commonly used by many Asian girls—especially in East Asia—to create a crease on their eyelids to enlarge the eyes. They applied makeup to create contours on their faces so that their noses sat higher and thinner and their faces appeared fairer and angled. Looking now at the ideals of Asian beauty across the continent, it is unsettling to see how similar they have come to resemble the Western ideal.

The Western standard of beauty has imparted a complicated relationship of self-image for Asian women. Many Asian American women have internalized the white ideal of what is beautiful in part because they have rarely seen a person of color—specifically, one who exhibits quintessential Asian features—depicted as being conventionally attractive. Plastic surgery then becomes a tempting option for some of these women in their quest to look more Western, which they believe will give them a competitive edge, more privilege, and social mobility in both their own culture and Western culture. Asian American women over time have begun to internalize that their features, straying so far from white beauty ideals, must render them less attractive. Asian American women commonly are dissatisfied with race-specific body parts such as the eyes, nose, and face shape, which differentiate them from white women and the white expectations of glamour.[43]

Beauty, always remaining close to the supposed worth of a woman, is given a particular kind of prominence in Asian culture. White skin and white women's features are pinnacles of beauty that are central to Asian standards, whether they are conscious of it or not. In Korean, Japanese, Chinese, and Indian cultures, where racial homogeneity presides, the meticulous ideal of beauty becomes exploited into a singular image that is then glamorized, sexualized, commodified, and exacerbated. But even before this paradigm of westernized Asian beauty was created in the twenty-first century, the image of oversexualized Asian women had started to take shape.

The Hypersexualization of Asian American Women

American mainstream culture and society at large have tended to desexualize and emasculate Asian male bodies, while Asian female bodies have been eroticized, hypersexualized, and underrepresented. This can be exemplified by the whitewashing of Asian American roles in film.[44] In 2015, Emma Stone played a woman of Hawaiian and Asian heritage in *Aloha*, and in 2017, Scarlett Johansson donned a cropped black wig in an iconic Japanese female role in *Ghost in the Shell*. This also happens to Asian American men who are cast poorly. For example, Mickey Rooney's role as Mr. Yunioshi in *Breakfast at Tiffany's* inaugurated the caricature of Asian men into the pop culture stratosphere. He, as a white man heavily squinting his eyes and speaking with an irreverent Japanese accent, propagated a socially strayed, irritated male and normalized the trivialization of Asians as comedic relief. Undoubtedly, there is no shortage of Asian American actors to play these parts. Casting white people to play Asian American characters validates a system that capitalizes on displaying minorities through a white lens, wherein they only work to add levity or stereotyped embellishments of Asian culture and heritage.

Asian American women have been seen as sexual objects due to racial stereotyping and contemporary distortions of Asian cultural understandings. When Asian men first arrived in the United States, they were feminized due to their traditional long pigtails and were offered traditional feminine work as dishwashers, cooks, and cleaners. On the other hand, Asian women were viewed as exotic foreign objects—prostitutes and sex workers who existed to be conquered for the sexual gratification of men. Thus where Asian men were emasculated, Asian women were hypersexualized.[45]

US immigration laws also made it nearly impossible for Asian women to come into the United States, as there was a deep-seated fear of Asian people reproducing and overrunning the American population. One outcome of this fear was the Immigration Act of 1924, barring Asians from entering the United States. Laws like this and societal attitudes shaped the gender composition and social class of Asian American communities in the United States. Even though married women had a difficult time entering the United States, single Asian women were brought in as sex workers. These women were sexually exploited by white men and then were disposed of when they caught venereal diseases. The perception of Asian women as sexual objects makes them expendable; they are viewed as commodities rather than as human beings.

White American culture perpetuates the hypersexualization of Asian American women as mere objects of sexual gratification. Cultural narratives found in movies like *Memoirs of a Geisha* and *Madame Butterfly* sustain the notion of Asian women as existing solely to fulfill and indulge male sexual desire. Other cultural artifacts, such as Psy's viral music video "Gangnam Style,"[46] also propagate the hypersexualization of Korean women, affirming westernized standards of beauty as superior. This practice needs to be challenged.

In addition, US militarization has played a role in cementing this perception. Scholars have argued that a critical transnational perspective needs to be adopted to see how Asian women's movement has impacted the legacy of the United States in the Asian Pacific.[47] The impact has been significant and continues to be so. The identity of Korean women has been frequently tied to the militarization of Korea, a process that has deepened and reinforced the portrayal of hypersexualized Korean women. The US military troops based in Korea have continuously viewed Korean women as sexual partners from whom they find sex and comfort. Many American men visited Korean brothels and ended up having children with Korean women. Some Korean women even became military brides and were brought to the United States after the war. Many of these military brides were only desired for sex, oftentimes treated horribly and suffered abuse. These military brides were known as *yanggongju*, which was colloquially translated as "the foreigner's whore."[48] These circumstances with the US military have created a certain behavior and attitude that continues to feed into the narrative of hypersexualized Korean women.

These cases and personal histories reveal how the hypersexualization of Korean American women manifested through literature, stereotyping, racism, and sexism. The complexity of Korean American women's identity—shaped by history, culture, militarization, colonialism, white supremacy—challenges us to discern what lies beneath the surface and what rustles in our peripheries. The overt sexualization of Asian American women is not just severely confining and demeaning but strikingly oppressive. Political, societal, and religious actions must be taken for the healing and liberation of all Asian American women who are marginalized in society.

Conclusion

Xenophobia, racism, and discrimination toward people of color are destructive forces in the Asian American community, leaving the community consciousness torn between two cultures and between prosperity and insecurity. At the same time, these forces of oppression have pushed many Asian Americans to work harder in all aspects of society. Asian Americans take pause and wonder if only we can overcome differences and begin to welcome and embrace one another. Differences enrich, improve, and strengthen our lives, becoming a thing to triumph rather than fear.

I believe we all need to embrace the other. We need to embolden ourselves in creating more dialogue, understanding, and acceptance not just with the dominant society but with other marginalized communities. Asian Americans have to see themselves as part of a larger community of color. We are often hoodwinked into believing the model minority story and that we should be grateful for our successes. Note that such gratitude, apparently compulsory, frames our interests in an unethically narrow fashion and invites a kind of political affiliation with whiteness. But the America of Blacks, Latinxs, Native Americans, Middle Easterners, and so on is also essential to our America. Thus, with a wider sense of ethical community, we can allow ourselves to not only listen to their pain but also acknowledge their efforts to overcome the sources of pain, by resistance, creativity, and power. We need to deconstruct and transform culture, rethinking our image of God and how we perceive God in our place and our world. This will help us achieve spiritual equality instead of clinging to an oppressive morality.

Understanding ourselves as Asian Americans is a seminal step toward overcoming some of the problems and barriers we face. Identity isn't prescriptive. Easy, ready-made categories or narratives can help you understand your place, even if you choose to reject them. We gain power by recognizing and understanding our struggles that are a result of outside forces.[49] As we unpack our history and hardships, we are motivated to create a better future.

In the flux of power, hope can provide the steady energy we need to propel us forward in life—not just during times of hardship and brokenness but during the times when we thrive. We need the ability to make decisions for ourselves rather than being coerced into action. We need the freedom to change our lives rather than act out of desperation. While the imbalance of power is natural to life's order, hope remains secure, silent and available throughout.

4

SEXISM

Home, Church, and Society

I first attended church at seven years old at the London First Korean Presbyterian Church in London, Ontario, Canada.

Without friends or many companions, my general uncomfortable demeanor around other kids grew into a helpless awkwardness. At school, I grew complacent in my silent existence, afraid of judgment, often going days at school without speaking at all for fear my accent or broken English would be mocked. No one saw me, and at the time, I reasoned it was better than being seen for the wrong, humiliating reasons. In my empty school days, I daydreamed. I made a habit of fantasizing about being a beautiful white woman—someone who didn't have to try to capture the attention of friends or strangers and naturally gained the adoration of others. In these dreams, I was celebrated, vibrant, and triumphant.

When I met Ms. Kim, a Korean neighbor, it seemed as though I bridged a gap between this fantasy and a more grounded reality. Young and beautiful, Ms. Kim was helpful to all the new Korean immigrants and trusted by the white people who had resided in the apartment complex for decades. My earliest memory of Ms. Kim was meeting her at the doorway of my apartment complex. I remember her long black hair shifting behind the glass as she waved at me excitedly as if she knew me. She swung open the door and called me over, and thinking I was in trouble, I wondered what I had done wrong. When I approached her, she knelt down, her dark eyes gleaming and her pale, round face glimmering with perspiration. She asked me if I wanted to play with some other Korean kids that lived in the building, she was treating them to some cold drinks and popsicles at her house. It was the first time I had been invited to someone else's home. It was also the first time I played with the kids in my building complex. Ms. Kim invited us kids over several times in the week, cooking us roasted nuts and peeling large platters of pears, happily giving all of our parents a much needed break. She encouraged all the kids in the building to become friends, and for the first time ever, I made a group of friends. This wasn't the only first with Ms. Kim however, because she also took me to church.

Surprisingly, while my parents were not Christian and had no desire to attend church, they did not stop their two young daughters from going to church with a woman who was basically a stranger to them. Back then, my parents trusted anyone who helped feed my sister and me, and they believed we would be safe with Ms. Kim. So every Sunday afternoon for two years, Ms. Kim drove us to church.

When we arrived, there were donuts. This was my first memory of church; it was the thing that drew me in and the thing that kept me coming back. Like jewels in a display case, several unassuming white boxes revealed glimmering glazed, cream-filled, jam-filled and raisin donuts. The sugarcoated twists were my favorite—I still associate Sunday mornings with the taste—so when I got the chance, I ate one right away and wrapped a second one in a napkin for Sunday school. After the service, we had a simple Korean meal of rice, various soups, some *banchan* (a variety of Korean side dishes made of marinated and fermented vegetables, fish, or meats), and of course, lots of kimchi. During these meals, we would sit with friends in the fellowship hall and socialize. Here, I shyly began to make the friends I have known all throughout my life.

For me, these simple rituals offered a rare refuge from the isolation that became commonplace in my regular life. In 1970s London, Ontario, I was faced with the constant reminder that I was alternative, novel, exotic, and peculiar. Whether I was at school or in the grocery store with my family, I felt my acute difference with every interaction. But at church, I was the norm; I was just like everyone else, speaking a hybrid lexicon of Korean and English. At church, I could be with people who looked like me, smelled like me, and ate the foods I ate. It was a deeply happy part of my childhood. Eventually, my parents saw how much we enjoyed our Sundays and our newfound dedication to this practice and decided to attend as well to see what all the fuss was about.

As I get older and reflect on it, I grow more aware of how this early formative experience of the church—riding in Ms. Kim's rickety car, licking sugar off my fingers, and sharing kimchi with other kids—formed my outlook and perspective of church. This ritual brought me the simple gift of communion, of kinship in a time when isolation crept into my every aspect of living. It was also the beginning of my spiritual awakening, marking the road map for the future of my faith journey. Church began as a place where I sought to find connection. Eventually, it became a place where I could offer others community.

As time went on, church began to define how my parents wanted my sister and me to spend our time. The church's most significant influence manifested through the impact of worship and fellowship, providing real, lasting friendships and vivid memories of coming to know God. The church is a refuge for so many who seek community—more specifically, for minorities who desire a common meeting place that encompasses fellowship, worship, family, education, culture, and economy.[1] For many immigrants, the church is where fragmented diasporas connect; in the church, immigrants can bond over their own food, converse in their own language, and share news of employment, their native homes, and their children's education. Church becomes an extended family for immigrants who have lost or left their families and experience discrimination in the larger community.

My parents couldn't find a place of acceptance in white Canadian society. They couldn't speak English well enough to ever have white friends with whom they could socialize, and ultimately, they never acclimated to non-Korean social life. This was not rare for many first-generation immigrants in the mid-1970s. All my parents' friends were either from church or from the wider Korean community. The church became an embracing ethnic cosmos that reminded them of their homeland—an escape from the larger community that was so distant to them. For immigrants, church can be more than a place of worship. Since we did not have any other family in Canada, the church members became our family, and church gatherings included birthday celebrations, graduation parties, and wedding receptions to which everyone was invited. In some sense, church became one large community where regular family events were extended to all members. However, just as families have complicated dynamics, power relations, and issues, so does the church.

Attending church was the beginning of my faith journey, when I began to understand myself, the world, and God. The racism, discrimination, and xenophobia embedded into my daily life were normalized, swiftly decreasing my self-worth as well the worth of other Korean, Chinese, and Vietnamese kids I grew up with. Helplessly, we tried to see ourselves reflected, but especially in each other, we found only mere echoes of insecurity. This insecurity, which should have been palliated, was deeply felt at church. The normalized discrimination—the effect of institutionalized racism and sexism—that existed at school took a different form at church, morphing into a fully mature, pious, rational kind of bigotry. Then the church was not a haven or an oasis from the difficulties of racism but a place that also practiced, exhibited, and harbored hatred.

My invisibility evolved from a form of self-protection to a more dangerous form of pacification, even comfort. It seemed to me that it was easier to exist passively. But now, I ask myself if it really was. What does it do to the human spirit to be invisible? What does it mean to be invisible? What do we lose as a society when we erase a group of people? This is the ongoing struggle I endured as a child growing up in the church: learning to recognize and validate my own value.

Many Churches in My Childhood

Even though our main church was the London First Korean Presbyterian Church, my dad decided to take my sister and me to other churches throughout the week. My dad was concerned that we were only immersed in a Korean subculture and were not getting exposed or better adjusted to white society. He thought of non-Korean churches as free English classes for his two daughters, fearing that we were falling behind in our language proficiency. He would take us to a small Baptist church for Sunday night services at 6:00 p.m. This church had a stoic, very old white pastor who welcomed us every week. The children would sit in a section of the small chapel singing songs for about twenty minutes before worship began. We would sing "What a Friend We Have in Jesus" every Sunday night, and as we sang, a warm smile spread across the pastor's face, revealing an old soul comforted by the music of children.

My dad took us to a larger Baptist church on Sunday mornings. Due to the Korean church attendance in the afternoon, we only went to the Baptist Sunday school classes. I remember my Sunday school teacher put snacks, mostly chips, into little sandwich baggies and tied them up with green twist ties. I couldn't wait for her to pass out the snacks, as these were things that my mom never bought for us. So Sunday school at the Baptist church was always associated with salty treats. I can still remember the joy of receiving the snack bag and savoring each piece, always leaving with the salty, satisfying seasoning in my mouth.

On Fridays, we went to the Missionary Alliance Community Church for fellowship nights. I have fond memories of playing Bible games, dodge ball, tag, and board games. We also had potluck dinners, which were a new phenomenon for me. I had no idea that people brought hoards of delicious goods in Tupperware containers just to share them with strangers. We even had "lucky dinners" where you bid on a dinner and eat the one you win without knowing what it is—one could say that every time I went to any church, I was somehow eating. I made a lot of new friends at this church, but more remarkably, I ended up growing attached to a young couple who had no children. They gave me a set of keys to their home and said I could come over anytime I wanted. I would go there anytime I was bored or lonely, talking with them, eating with them, and just letting the time pass as I watched TV in their family room.

These associations to various churches during the week were all part of my dad's great plan for my sister and me to become more Canadian. For me, though, they sparked a desire to learn more about Christianity and the God that was preached about within the church walls.

Utilitarian Church

My parents converted to Christianity from Buddhism as they began to attend the Presbyterian church Ms. Kim introduced us to. My sister and I enjoyed attending church, and my parents enjoyed not having to entertain us or cook for us at any point during the day.

My parents were both from Buddhist families in Korea. Their relatives were not strong believers in Buddhism, but by cultural inertia, my parents grew up conforming to Buddhist culture. When they immigrated to Canada, they never went to a Buddhist temple or practiced Buddhism. Like many Korean immigrants, they slowly decided to check out the Christian church, mostly out of a need for community. Many of their friends began to attend church and kept asking my parents to attend. Eventually, church was presented to them as the hottest place in town. So after going once in a while to check it out or pick my sister and me up, they grew to be loyal attendees. Two years after first stepping into church, my parents converted to Christianity.

Converting to Christianity and attending church became a survival mechanism for Korean immigrants. It was a natural progression for many of them, both wanting and feeling pressured to meet and socialize with other Koreans and find information about employment, businesses, and survival strategies in their new country. It was also a place to teach their children the Korean language and history through a Korean school operated by the church on Saturdays. Even further, at church, parents gained valuable information about how they could better help their young children thrive in the new country.

My parents soon enjoyed going to church. It was a good thing for them. They found a vital missing piece in their lives that was abandoned in their move: family, friends, and true solidarity with others like them. Going to church filled their hunger for community and helped them overcome some of the regrets, fears, and hardships of living in a new country without many resources.

Conservative Church

The Korean Presbyterian church that we attended when I was a child went through a division in the mid-1980s. When the congregation separated into two churches, my parents decided to attend the smaller church. They thought the smaller church was more family-like and would allow them to be seen as individuals rather than merely numbers within a larger church body.

Looking back, this wasn't the best choice for me. I lost the opportunity to play with my many Korean friends on Sunday. If one did not attend the same church, it was harder to maintain friendships. Our new church only had a small youth group, so I was stuck hanging around a small handful of friends, while the other church had a huge youth group with the opportunity to broaden social circles and get involved with more clubs and leadership positions.

My parents' church was a conservative evangelical church. This had a huge impact on my sister and me. Since we attended a conservative church, there were many things we were not allowed to do while we were growing up: We were not allowed to listen to the radio, as non-Christian songs were songs of the devil. We were not allowed to go shopping on Sunday, as it was a holy day. We were not allowed to attend dances, as dancing was too sexual. We were not allowed to smoke or drink, which were activities that we did not have the capacity to be interested in anyway, seeing as how we were never around cigarettes or alcohol. This pietism and conservativism infiltrated every aspect of our lives, but most prominently, it infiltrated our understanding of gender roles. Gender expectations as governed by the church were strict. The women were relegated to the kitchen to cook meals and prepare snacks and donuts. If there was a midweek church gathering, the women were expected to organize and put together a meal for the occasion. This preparation also meant shopping, cooking, and serving the primarily male congregation—in other words, women performed domestic-like work. The men, on the other hand, were the leaders in the church.

Though neither type of work is innately negative, the hazard comes in the ways that this norm formatively shapes ideas of oneself, one's place in society (as a woman or a man), and one's gender performance (how one behaves in relation to their understanding of their gender). For me, it encouraged a harshly self-critical period of my young adult life where I constantly questioned the value of anything I did if I was only going to be pushed into domestic and childbearing duties.

Sexism in the Church

Asian American women are influenced by Western philosophy, culture, and religious customs. Many of the practices within the churches these women attend have been created by Western ideologies and traditions. Catholic, Lutheran, Anglican/Episcopal, Reformed, Presbyterian, Methodist, and Baptist churches were all born and developed to maturity in Italy, Spain, France, Germany, Bohemia, Holland, and England. Only Pentecostalism, famous for its generous welcoming of both Blacks and women from the day it was founded, bears any traces of minority fingerprints.

Even though the church was a positive force in my life, the stringent conservatism regarding gender combined with the sexism present in Korean culture also made it a negative force. Many Koreans intended to hold on to the societal norms that made them feel comfortable in an otherwise uncomfortable foreign land. Mixing Korean gender expectations and conservative Christian understanding of women bred toxic patriarchy and lowered the self-esteem of many women in the church.

Many church activities were split by gender. There was the women's Bible study group and then the men's Bible study group. Women cooked and cleaned in the kitchen, while the men led in church and attended session and deacon's meetings. The women ate together after church as they sat around tables and gossiped. The men sat at their own tables and talked about church and work. It was obvious to me that there was a clear division of labor and strict rules concerning the interaction between men and women in the church. These inequitable expectations, stemming from Confucian backgrounds, are still evident in the Korean global church today. Since Confucianism was introduced to Korea in 372 CE, it has been embedded in Korean culture, history, society, and philosophy. It is difficult to divorce Confucianism from new Korean religious practices because it is such a fundamental part of the Korean ethos, behavior, and understanding.

Despite this, the church did provide some solace for immigrant men and women. It gave them a sense of family, hope, and acceptance. Some male immigrants (women rarely attended college) were graduates from top universities in Korea with professional degrees in medicine, engineering, law, and music. Some were able to overcome the language barrier and find employment in their respective fields. But many others were not so lucky. Thus, many families had to begin from the bottom. The work was significantly below their educational standing back home. Some didn't share with their children that they had to do menial jobs such as janitorial work; many were ashamed that their lives had come to this. The church became an uplifting place where these men were offered the same level of dignity and status as their peers. Many men held leadership roles they would never be able to attain in the dominant white society. They became deacons, elders, pastors, choir directors, and other kinds of leaders. Many Korean male immigrants overcame their fears and thrived in such positions of leadership. But of course, this came at a cost for women. Because the men wanted to continue to hold these positions of power within the church, they excluded women. Those who were a part of my mother's generation didn't question this arrangement. They had lived in the patriarchal culture in Korea and saw their new lives as a natural continuation of the old. But for the younger children and teens, it was far less comfortable during a cultural time when women were actively fighting for equality, continuing the work that second-wave feminists began during the sixties.

Though I see this early time in the church as a period of rebirth, connection, and learning, in the margins of these milestones are the beginnings of a declining feminine confidence. I saw the roles laid out for me, and yet I kept wondering whether the traditional feminine gender roles represented the life that I and all the other girls were destined for.

My Ordination

I was a candidate for ordination for eighteen years. This is an unusually long time, as most are candidates for only a few months. I didn't plan it that way, but between having children, moving to a different country and teaching in a seminary, my ordination got delayed. Once I started the process again, it took several years. I had to take two ordination exams for the Presbyterian Church (USA), though they exempted me from two other exams. I also had to preach and become a candidate for ordination. Finally, when everything was done and I was ready, I decided to get ordained in the Korean Presbyterian church where I was working part time.

The minister of the Korean church where I worked decided to delay my ordination by a couple of months. A few weeks before my ordination, he approached me. We exchanged small talk, and when I brought up my ordination, his demeanor changed. He told me that at any time, he could prevent my ordination from happening. I didn't understand. I asked what he meant, but he only repeated his statement and walked away. Dumbfounded, I wondered why my ordination was dependent on his decision, as it was already approved by the presbytery. I also wondered why this development discomforted him so much. I wasn't planning to work at his church as his associate pastor, but somehow the very fact of my upcoming ordination threatened and troubled him.

A few days before my ordination, the minister began questioning me about wearing a robe, saying that I didn't really need a minister's robe or even an announcement in the church bulletin about the ordination service. He claimed that these things were all frivolous add-ons and that if I was serious about ordination, I wouldn't need any of them. Though I questioned him in the beginning, I eventually became reticent and just let him continue to tell me what I didn't need—or more suggestively, what I didn't deserve.

Three days before my ordination, after another belittling conversation with the minister, my skin began to break out in hives, a way that my body reacts to enormous stress. I thought to myself that perhaps I should not go through with it. Perhaps I should put it off until the situation improved. But I stuck it through and went to church on November 13, 2011, to get ordained. In Presbyterian ordination, a commissioning service follows the event. I sat next to the minister, and he turned to me and asked, "Do we have to go through with the commissioning too?" I was flabbergasted and could not believe he was still trying to prevent the ordination service from happening. I just rolled my eyes and turned my back toward him so I could just get through the commissioning part of my ordination service.

A few years after my ordination, I went to speak in Myanmar. In one of my lectures, a Korean feminist theologian, Chung Hyun Kyung, came with her students to hear me speak. After my talk, a few students asked me questions about ordination, and I shared the difficulties I had faced during the process. Chung Hyun Kyung listened attentively to my ordination story and asked me, "Do you know why you had such a difficult time?" I said no. She said, "Because the moment you were ordained, you became more equal to him. He did not want to support your professional rise. He wanted you to be obedient to him and remain the same." A few other women in the audience recalled experiences where they met similar tensions with male leaders in the church, particularly as they grew into leadership positions. While I was not shocked, I realized I hadn't understood the breadth of sexism in the church, especially when progress and inclusivity were at the forefront of many church discussions. We have come a long way since then, but we still have a long way to go.

Western Patriarchy in the Church

As we analyze patriarchy today, we must be aware of its pervasive presence in churches. We recognize that patriarchy is no longer restricted to the power of the father over his kinship group; it is defined by the social structures and ideologies that have enabled men to dominate and exploit women throughout recorded history.[2] In church history, popes, bishops, and priests were exclusively male.

Women were theologically and biblically viewed as second-class citizens who could be easily dominated or subjugated. The church not only did this to its own but also effectively shaped secular thought and contemporary society, systematically oppressing women by effect.

Patriarchy is the exploitation and victimization on the basis of gender and sex; it is defined and framed within the terms of male-female gender dualism, which favors men over women. In the confines of patriarchy, the difference between male and female is considered to be the most basic and essential difference of humanity. It is the origin and basis of all other divisions—of economic class, culture, race, religion, nationality, and age. Men's domination over women and women's exclusion from politics, culture, history, and religion have been the norm throughout much of history, which has relegated women to domesticity—a life separated from outside society and contained inside the home, purposed to serve the family.[3] This domination of women also occurred in the church for most of church history; however, its presence in the Asian American church in relation to historic Asian patriarchal culture demands an exploration of how such a relationship reinforces patriarchy in the wider Western church.

Western patriarchy was mediated and perpetuated through Christianity, the dominant Western religion, for almost two thousand years. Both the Old Testament and the New Testament portray God and Christ in patriarchal terms and, in turn, defined how men and women were to be in the church and in society at large. If men were more closely representative of the Divine, then it was clearly believed that men can rule over women, just as how God rules over humanity. Through influential theologians such as Augustine and Aquinas, the highly accepted Aristotelian view of the inferior human "natures" of slaves and freeborn women became woven into Christian theology's basic fabric, doctrine, and practice.[4] The influence of the Aristotelian view of women was extensive, embedding itself into the New Testament writings and letters that have been used to teach, indoctrinate, and mold Christian believers' ways of thinking, acting, and worshipping. The church, which was formed and sustained by women and men alike, came to codify, embed, breed, and legitimize patriarchy and sexism. For the Korean church in America, sexism became further amplified through the Confucian lens and common cultural practices that permeated the Asian consciousness.

Women and Church

Women occupy male spaces. This is a difficult reality for any young girl to reconcile with as she seeks a life of equality and freedom. Churches are no different, as women try their best to thrive and find peace in a space that has been imbued with patriarchy, a structure that upholds the church pews, walls, and pulpit. In such an environment, women can feel intensely divided and alienated from God. In the very institution that is meant to offer sacred community, safety, and support, women have often faced degradation at the hands of male church leadership. The church space should reflect the life of Jesus, who welcomed women and lifted them up even as the patriarchal society tried to shun women as sinners and prostitutes. When a group of men was going to stone a woman caught in an act of adultery, Jesus said, "Let anyone among you who is without sin be the first to throw a stone at her" (John 8:7). Jesus was trying to show that everyone is a sinner and that Jesus will not condemn us (8:11). Jesus loves all of us, men and women; we should do likewise, especially in the church. Women should be able to practice their gifts of the Spirit and teach, preach, lead, and minister. Women in the church should not occupy male spaces; rather, the church should create space for both women and men to occupy equally.

Just as Confucianism influences the lives and identities of Korean American women, so do Christianity and the church. The Korean American church predominantly reflects the key characteristics of traditional Korean culture: it is conservative, hierarchical, and male dominated. The Korean American church continues to marginalize women and strengthens a patriarchal church structure through misinterpreted Scripture and male eulogization. They are not to hold authority over men, and thus women are not easily welcomed to the pulpit and places of teaching, preaching, and power. If men continue to dominate most of the positions of power, there is no doubt that some women will feel as though they are merely secondary counterparts. The women's rights movement needs to be translated into the practices of Korean American churches so that Korean American women can also be viewed as equal in leadership and ministerial roles. Korean churches lag behind dominant, often white churches and thus have a longer road to travel to achieve gender equality.

In Korean American women's daily lives, all the divergent spaces they occupy—may it be their houses, workplaces, or churches—are unified through their interactions with them. Women move through one place to the next, existing as if they are somehow separate. Yet they bring the same spirit everywhere they go, bringing with them also their complicated feelings and lived experiences to every new place. What Korean American women endure at home goes on in church, and what goes on in church is transferred to the workplace.

Church has proven to be an essential community for immigrants, especially Korean American immigrants, as 71 percent attend church, which is much higher than the national average of 39 percent.[5] One of the typical questions Korean Americans ask when they first meet one another is "Which church do you attend?" With this opener, they can begin to initiate a longer conversation regarding their activities at church, their family's and friends' connections to the community, and how they can stay in touch in the future. However, this exchange must be translated. The question is not actually "Which church do you attend?" but really "Where do you belong?"

For Korean Americans attending church, the institution has four major sociological functions. First, churches provide fellowship for Korean immigrants and serve as social centers for meeting people and making friends. They help immigrants adjust to the host society by giving them valuable social services and information.[6] Churches provide various tools to navigate dominant society, as new immigrants typically feel isolated, insecure, lonely, and overwhelmed. Second, churches serve as centers of education—of the English language, North American culture, and biblical knowledge. Churches continue to run Korean language schools for the children of immigrants and for the wider community for anyone who is interested in learning Korean. Almost every Korean church has these language schools to teach the children Korean language, culture, and history. When I attended Korean language school, I learned traditional fan dancing and other cultural elements I would not have had access to otherwise. Third, churches confer social status and positions of leadership upon adult members. This is important for men, since it gives them leadership roles that are difficult to obtain within the dominant white American society. Fourth, churches reflect the traditional Confucian Korean cultural/ social structure and system. They are places where people can come together and reinforce their ethnic identity. Churches strengthen the Korean identity of immigrants by maintaining their cultural traditions.[7] Thus churches fulfill many of the social and psychological needs of immigrants; however, they also perpetuate the suffering of women by restricting females' roles and participation. For women in the immigrant community, the church has also been, in many ways, a center of contradiction—a place where they go to seek community and intellectual and spiritual nourishment but also experience systematic domination and oppression.

Women's leadership or authority was not fully accepted in Korean immigrant churches during most of the twentieth century, and the roles women were allowed to play were largely limited to being assistants to men. There is, however, an honorary position reserved for experienced church women called *kwonsa*. *Kwonsa* do not hold any decision-making power in the church, and this is basically a position for elderly Korean women who cannot be ordained elders in a Presbyterian church due to their gender.[8] When my own mother became a *kwonsa* in the church, she felt it was the highest honor she could receive. There was a big service followed by a banquet, recognition, gifts, and flowers. It was a huge celebration, and I remember my mother looking the happiest I had ever seen her. She knew she would hold no power with this position, but in her mind, the honor would suffice, and she would be fulfilled as a woman of faith in the church.

Hence women's roles and status in the Korean church as well as the Korean immigrant church share many Confucian and Yi dynasty society parallels, primarily seen in the attitude toward gender roles and filial duties. It does not really matter the denomination—whether Protestant or Catholic—women's roles are limited, and most churches will not accept women's ordination. Women have been excluded from many important roles and leadership positions but are allowed to serve as invisible helpers behind the scenes.[9] They are mainly relegated to kitchen-related services, which means that women repeat the daily routines of housework when they go to church on Sundays. Therefore, in many respects, the Korean American church systematically justifies the devaluation and subordination of women, as the church continues to be ruled by Confucian and patriarchal Christian notions of gender hierarchy, replicated with layers of cultural standards established back in Korea.[10]

When white missionaries first arrived in Korea, they taught patriarchal theology and church practices. Koreans continued these practices without much change even though some white churches slowly accepted women's ordination and welcomed them into leadership roles. Korean immigrant churches held fast to the 1960s' perception of women and didn't really change from their early immigrant days during the large wave of Korean immigration in the 1970s.

Most Korean North American women in the church accept and adjust to this Korean-Christian social environment. In such cases, the Christian God is seen as legitimatizing female inferiority, which leads women to accept the given social reality. Korean male pastors continue to teach and preach on biblical passages that align with Confucian teachings such as the following: "Wives, be subject to your husbands as you are to the Lord. For the husband is the head of the wife just as Christ is the head of the church" (Eph 5:22–23) and "Women should be silent in the churches. For they are not permitted to speak, but should be subordinate, as the law also says" (1 Cor 14:34). The Confucian teachings that subordinate women permeate Korean society, culture, and history and are reinforced in Korean Christianity. As a result, Korean American women try to live their Christianity in accordance with the elements of Korean culture that dictate that women are, or should be, inferior to men by nature and social function.

For my mother, the church was everything. Her friends were the ladies at church. Her weekends were spent at the church. She went to the daily prayer gatherings at 6:00 a.m. and the midweek services. She also cooked for the church and gave large offerings and donations. Her entire life was centered on the church. She would dress up only for church. She enjoyed all the different revival services. She revered her pastor as a human representation of pure morality, virtuosity, and righteousness.

At the time, women didn't have the freedom to explore or understand their call to ministry or what it meant to become a preacher or leader within a church. This was true for my mother as well. She was very gifted, but she never considered anything more than helping out in the church kitchen. She could not imagine herself as a leader or a preacher, as she faithfully obeyed the men in her life, be it her husband, her brother, or her pastor. She did everything she was told to do, like a good servant. This was very difficult for me to watch while growing up, as I wanted her to develop her faith, become a leader in the church, be independent, and even challenge her pastor rather than blindly follow him. As a whole, women from her generation couldn't challenge the reality they found themselves in, as their immersion within Korean culture often meant that their intellectual and spiritual needs were to be quieted, privatized, and repressed. Such patriarchy starved the feminine church collective.

Sexism during My Studies

Long before I decided to get married, everyone around me knew of my intentions to get my PhD. I didn't know exactly in what degree—theology or psychology—but I knew that I wanted to take my education as far as I could go.

When I became engaged, and then married, my in-laws were satisfied with their daughter-in-law studying for a higher degree, or so I thought. However, tensions started to rise between my sister-in-law and me. It became clear that she, and apparently the rest of her family, were keeping their disappointment quiet regarding my desire for further education. In fact, she felt as if my education was a burden on her family and that they could not speak candidly to me about my future life—which they actually wanted to limit to bearing children—because the prospect of school got uncomfortably in the way. My desire to go to school competed with my in-laws' desire to quickly have grandchildren. This conflict made me feel as though it was selfish for me to study during marriage and child-rearing age, when in reality, it was a sacrifice I had to make every day to not spend more time with my loved ones.

The attacks became more frequent and hostile, as I was not fulfilling the role of a traditional daughter-in-law—someone who was a quiet, obedient, stay-at-home mom. Even though I am one year older than my sister-in-law, I was understood as her junior, as I married the second son. It became so hostile that my brother-in-law eventually told me over the phone, "Since you are the youngest in our family, you have no choice but to obey us."

It became apparent to me that they were not happy with my studies or my independence. As the hostility grew, the more distant and withdrawn I became with my in-laws.

But what occurs in the home transfers elsewhere. Other Asian male students I encountered who knew of my predicament told me to quit my PhD studies—as if my degree meant nothing to me. They thought that as a newly married woman, I had an obligation to stay home and raise children. They wanted to keep women inside, residents of a domestic life rather than a professional or academic one, just as women were during Confucian times in Korea. I found ancient Confucian teachings embedded all around me.

One incident stands out. One day as I was eating in the seminary cafeteria, one of my Korean male classmates sat down in front of me. We started a congenial conversation, talking about our classes and how our work was coming along. Then, out of the blue, he said, "God would be happier if you had one baby rather than ten PhD degrees!" This man had just said to my face what countless others were saying about me behind my back. I went home feeling stunned that someone felt entitled to say this to me. Even though I was an adult and self-assured in what I wanted out of my life, my worth was still relegated to having children and caring for a family. It made me feel that everything I was going after, the sacrifices I knew I needed to make to get my degree, were not going to be respected in the eyes of my colleagues and my community. I became the first Korean woman to graduate with a PhD in theology at the University of Toronto—an accomplishment I'm immensely proud of, but it wasn't something some of my colleagues necessarily encouraged of me.

In immigrant communities, the burdens and limitations of Confucian philosophy are still visible within the home, church, and work and are seen as legitimized by Christianity and its Bible. Korean American women's navigation in this climate becomes complicated as they confront the biases of their old culture as well as their new American culture. Korean American women live with much anguish, pain, and sorrow. Their personal desires to escape oppressive elements of Confucian culture are not fulfilled, as those elements immigrated with them. Unable to assimilate into the dominant group, they are marginalized and minoritized by the dominant white society. While the church offered so much to Korean immigrants, Christianity did not do much to improve these women's circumstances. If anything, it exacerbated them.

From the beginning, Christianity portrayed God as masculine. As a result, men appear closer to God than women and, hence, believe they are better equipped to know the will of God. This type of misunderstanding legitimized patriarchy within the church to the detriment of women's health and spirituality. The Korean American church is no exception to the maleness of God. It is even more emphatic in its understanding and portrayal of a male God. Korean prayers, liturgy, and Sunday worship are so male centered that the presider and preacher will continuously call God "Father God." As a result, Korean American women struggle to find their own identity in the Christian church.

In many ways, Korean Christianity in the immigrant church communities has become problematic to women who want to develop their full humanity and improve their status through formal education. As a result, those women who view themselves as "good Christians" develop double selves in order to fit into two social environments, the church and the world outside the church. The Korean Christian culture in North America seems to perpetuate the image of women as an extension of men.[11] Yet despite all the negative consequences for women, they still attend the church.

Korean American women's experiences in society and the church have been largely defined by the confinement, disruption, and inhibition of sexism and racism. Racism has been experienced in wider society in the form of dangerous stereotypes, xenophobia, and discrimination. This societal attitude has had grave psychological consequences and forced many Korean American women into an identity crisis.[12]

Much of the Confucian understanding of obedience has infiltrated churches in Korea and the United States. Women are expected to be obedient, and the gender roles are more clearly defined, as many congregations are still resistant to women leaders or pastors. Many who attend a Korean American church experience grave sexism embedded within Korean history, culture, and society that manifests itself in church society and teaching. Furthermore, white Christianity itself has always been patriarchal, with its male language about God and how the church has viewed women as secondary citizens. Therefore, the double marginalization from Korean culture and white patriarchal Christianity has subordinated and oppressed Korean American women.

The condition of being in the margins affects the individual, their community, and their church. Thus Korean American women have two battles to fight: racism and sexism. In such a marginalized state, religious belongingness may provide strength for many Korean American women. As a whole, Asian American women need to retrieve and share our stories to help theologically reflect the female Asian American experience to create a dynamic understanding of Korean American women in the church. We need to self-reflect, understand our invisibility, and write and share our own stories. It is critical that we do so to excavate the wider history of our contributions and our necessity in this world in order to expand the roles we play within the progressing church and society.

As Korean American women search for a sense of belonging, their traditional understanding of God, as well as the heteronormative understandings of their gendered selves, must be challenged.

In order to do this, they need to dispute the center: the center of whiteness and the center of maleness.

The Church's Male God

In the myriad churches I attended as a child, God was always described as an old, white male sitting up in the clouds looking down as he ruled us mortal beings. I thought God had made women so that men had companions—someone to love, someone to care for and look after them. Even in my thoughts, men were central. It was a strange feeling to grow up thinking that despite being the main character in my story, I was destined to be a secondary character in the greater story. I was indoctrinated so heavily in the patriarchal stories of the Bible that I believed the only path I could possibly take to have a fulfilled, righteous life led to marriage, children, and domestic work.

I grew up thinking that I had to wear dresses to church, maintain a smile, greet everyone warmly but never too warmly, involve myself in the right activities, and take charge in the right circumstances—but never lead; that was the man's job. I watched my mother not be able to fight back when my father came down on her; his insistence that he was the head of the family, the ruler, was not just tolerated but accepted and justified. Just as God was the ruler over us, God had placed men on earth to be rulers over women. A man could do as he pleased, abusing, using, and silencing his wife if he wished to. My mother suffered in silence, and her two daughters watched helplessly, dying to speak out and hold their own.

The center of white privilege and white supremacy can be challenged by reimagining Korean American women's understanding of the Christian God. The maleness and whiteness of the Christian God need to be dismantled if racism and sexism are to be eliminated. Korean American women can begin to participate in such actions by dialoguing and engaging the Bible from a perspective of feminist theology that reimagines God in feminine terms. One necessary step is to understand God using wisdom language as found in Scripture.

To work toward equality, religious discourse, categories and languages about God, and nongendered forms and concepts must be elevated in our study and examination. This work must occur for women in the church to be liberated and equal. Korean American women who are theologically more conservative than white women will find this study to be a challenge. But it needs to occur with respect to the individual, slowly and rigorously. Only then will the church evolve its language and culture of male dominance. Language forms our thoughts and our ideas. Therefore, we cannot achieve any level of equality between men and women if our language about God remains masculine. The liberation of God language from masculinity will help work toward Korean American women's liberation in the church.

Sophia Christology or Wisdom Christology has been around since the Early Church, but it was slowly discarded and pushed away from our church history and doctrine. The elimination of Sophia Christology is evident today, as most churches focus on Logos Christology, which is the masculine understanding of God. A new retrieval of Sophia God may help us understand God in more feminine terms, which will be inclusive and empowering for all women around the globe. This will be most helpful to Korean American women, who suffer greatly from sexism in the church and in the wider society.

Sophia is the Greek word for "wisdom," and *Hokmah* is the Hebrew word for "wisdom." Wisdom is often associated with God in the Scriptures.[13] Proverbs has several passages that relate to wisdom, such as Proverbs 4:6–7: "Do not forsake her, and she will keep you; love her, and she will guard you. The beginning of wisdom is this: Get wisdom, and whatever else you get, get insight." We all need wisdom, as it will keep us and protect us. There are other scriptural passages that associate wisdom with God. Proverbs 2:6 says, "For the Lord gives wisdom; from his mouth come knowledge and understanding," and Daniel 2:20 states, "Blessed be the name of God from age to age, for wisdom and power are his." This association of God with wisdom and wisdom as female is a right step toward understanding God in feminine terms. With this, Korean American women can work toward a more liberative theology and presence in the church that embraces the femininity of God. Though understanding God in gendered terms such as feminine and masculine is not necessary, it does help us understand

and contextualize the abstractness of God. As God embodies the stable, unified harmony we strive to understand and embody, we must acknowledge that this means God's definition between feminine and masculine is one of total equality.

Another way to challenge the maleness of God is to embrace a Spirit God. The term for Spirit found in the Hebrew Scriptures is *ruach*, which is a feminine term. A Spirit God moves away from the male-gendered God that continuously reinforces patriarchy and sexism. Furthermore, a Spirit God understanding moves us away from a "white" Christian God. If God is not embodied in a white male body, then it becomes easier for Korean American women to embrace a God who seeks gender and racial equality.[14] To embrace a Spirit God means to refocus our understanding of God, which will lead to a fuller and universal understanding of God. In addition, embracing a Spirit God means embracing the Korean heritage and culture, which already has an understanding of Spirit God with the Asian term *Chi*. Chi means "wind," "energy," and "breath" and serves the same function as *ruach* in the Old Testament and *pneuma* in the New Testament. Embracing an understanding of a Spirit God will work toward eliminating a sexist and racist church, as it opens our eyes to an inclusive and loving God.

As Korean American women fight against racial and gender injustice, they must reimagine historical Christian teachings about God. As this occurs, they can begin to experience the wholeness that comes from a Spirit God who embraces all people regardless of race, gender, sexuality, or socioeconomic status. Then perhaps Korean American women can feel a sense of radical belonging in this world that has always kept them confined as perpetual foreigners. They can also begin to push for multiple centers rather than one dominant white center. In this way, people can coexist and feel welcomed and embraced. As Korean American women live in new hybrid spaces, hybridity can be a source of reimagining home, something they have long been seeking and something that is necessary for positive forward progression. We need to encourage women's leadership in the church and work toward dismantling the patriarchy that makes women's presence in the church invisible.

Conclusion

The church is our spiritual home, the place we come to nourish our minds and spirits and take rest from the outside world. Yet, like our own homes, they harbor the same creaks, flaws, and things in need of repair. The sexism embedded in our churches eats away at the very framework of our spiritual home, loosening the structure and endangering the occupants. Sexism has been present in the church from the beginning of its organization and endures today. While some churches have been able to begin ordaining women to the ministry, there are still many denominations that refuse to do so. The church needs to recognize its own flaws and come to terms with its patriarchy if it is to be meaningful to women today.

5

LIVING INTO A THEOLOGY
OF VISIBILITY

In my personal life, I find a growing determination to become more
visible as an Asian American woman. US policies were imposed on
Asian Americans to make them second-class citizens. These policies
served to both systemically institutionalize and encourage racism,
xenophobia, and marginalization and led to the stereotyping of
Asian Americans in society. For Asian American women, Asian and
Western cultures compound and strip them of their visibility.

Occupying a marginal space, I wake to the dynamics of my
spiritual growth through long-hidden wisdom found in the various liminal communities I inhabited. I became more aware of the
interrelations of my formation and re-formation within these over-
lapping social contexts; in turn, this has invited me to find peace
in the fluctuations of my identity and cultural communities and,
even further, to find power in them. While it is a challenge, it also

allowed me to be invited by the Spirit to gain the confidence in my visibility to be a voice against sexism, racism, and every other oppressive praxis.[1]

My journey has not been easy, and it is not over. My lifelong struggle with societal visibility has damaged my well-being and tested my spirituality in ways that I could seldom deal with on my own. Invisibility obscures our understanding of self—our desires, our perceptions. This is the burden that Asian Americans, especially women, carry with us, but our oppression can be lifted by decentering the dominant frame of reference in which we operate within the Christian world: white male Euro-theology. White male Euro-theology determined and defined Asian American women's space and identity. It led to the internalization of false identities that were created for us to be subordinate and subservient to white patriarchy as it endured in the image of a white male God. The mythos of the white male God has had immense consequences for communities of women of color. Thus, we must acknowledge the ways in which we may have unconsciously embedded dominant falsehoods as truth and reimagine an innovated, liberative Christianity that will embrace the flourishing of all lives equivalently. Decentering is a joint endeavor. It happens as we seek the Spirit of God to lead us on the path to liberation. Such a change is shaped by the Spirit, as the community of the Trinity works to further the original intent of creation as a mutually beneficial kin-dom where all people are welcomed and embraced by the Spirit of God. The burden to give voice and visibility to this vision arises from and is embedded in our blood, our bodies, and our histories. It is in the air that Asian American women breathe; it is part of who we are. It inspires and instructs us to express our valued identities visibly, resisting and reforming the dynamics in our societies that perpetuate invisibility. A theology of visibility using Asian concepts and ideas liberates Asian Americans and works toward freeing all people made invisible.

A Dangerous Theology

Much of Christian theology has been dangerous to people of color, and Asian American women have been no exception. Some of the unjust teachings of racism in the church are fueled by white male theologies that perpetuate white superiority and maintain the status quo. Those in power thus use theology to manipulate others into maintaining the social hierarchy: whites are at the top, and people of color are at the bottom; men are superior to women, and women cannot hold leadership positions. Therefore, due to the danger of white theologies, it is important to unpack them so we can recognize the need for a theology of visibility.

In much of Christian history, white male theology has supported the domination of women, colonialism of Asian countries, immigration restrictions against Chinese, the internment of Japanese Americans during World War II, and xenophobic actions against Asian Americans. Christians have misused Scripture, theology, and sociology to maintain inequality, and many Christians have sustained these ideas. For this reason, it is crucial that we examine and understand the dominant white male European theology to uncover where we have come and where we must go.

White Male European Theology

As an immigrant child growing up in Canada, I learned quickly that I was not expected to speak. I remember the sudden surprise of the people in the room when I would open my mouth to mention something, and sometimes, even I would be startled if another Asian chose to speak up. If there was one thing I grasped as a young Korean immigrant, it was that white men weren't just the chosen leaders and thinkers of society; they were the chosen speakers as well. I was accustomed to the white men who were so inclined to speak on my behalf, who were empowered and enlightened enough to teach me the "truth" of Jesus and God. It was ingrained into my and other immigrants' subconscious and led to the misguided belief in the Asian Christian community that white knowledge, theology, and spirituality were far greater than anything we had ever possessed.

As I reflect on my own childhood, I cannot help but understand my experiences in relation to white male European theology and Eurocentrism. Everything white was good, and everything that fell outside of it—my inherited Asian culture and Korean spirituality—was inferior, savage, or evil. Therefore, it was necessary to expunge nonwhiteness from my personal, social, and congregational life.

Theology is an experience of God in culture from one's personal and contextual point of view. In our comprehension of God, we reflect on our experiences, our praxis, and our cultural context to come to a deeper understanding of how God's presence is felt on earth. God appears not just to white men but to all people. Asian American women experience God as Chi in our being, as Chi gives us energy in a racist and oppressive society that saps our strength. We need to see how our visions of God change our actions and how we ought to live our lives as Chi flows through us and offers vitality to others, allowing us to exist with *jeong*[2] and community.

The oppression of Asian Americans is often a consequence of white arrogance rather than any particular character flaw. White Christian arrogance is learned and legitimized and rendered as the foundational norm within a society embedded in racism. Just as liberation from patriarchy is for both women and the men who oppress them, liberation from white supremacy is for both Asian Americans and the whites who continue to oppress them.

Along with steps to decenter white patriarchal theology, it is pertinent to understand ourselves in relation to others. Understanding the developments and origins of identity will help us engage in moving the margins and, as a result, moving and dismantling our own marginality. Trinh T. Minh-ha understands identity as a means of redeparting.[3] This means that in order to understand one's identity, one needs to return to a denied heritage, which will allow one to start again with different departures, pauses, and arrivals. For Asian American women, the suppressed heritage is the preservation of Asian culture within local Chinatowns, Koreatowns, Japantowns, Vietnam enclaves, and the church. Asian heritage is even more denied in theology, as the dominant white theology continually restates that Asian culture, identity, and heritage are unnecessary and diminutive for the majority society in America. Denials result in relegating Asian American women to "the other." When a person is made the other, they are put in a class with fewer privileges; to make someone the other is to diminish them to a marginal class.

As Euro-American supremacy continues to hold theology as its very own, we recognize its participation in racism, sexism, and the marginalization of Asian American women. Consequently, it is now long overdue to open theology's door. In doing so, we allow the rich beauty of global voices to enter the theological house. Theology can become a place of multiple centers—the complex orbit it always presented itself to be—where all the different voices are dignified, upheld, and understood.

Decentering

Eurocentric theology is centered on whiteness. White people have defined, developed, published, and stated what theology is. Such an institution of theology has become insulated, bounded by the perceptions and orientations of white men who possess the ability to encounter the religious global body and uplift shifting religious centers. In an ever-globalizing world, we must become creators of a progressive theology—one that requires all voices and diverse interests to be welcomed in a spiritual enterprise from which we can all learn, heal, and find peace.

Along with steps to decenter theology, it is pertinent to understand our own identity in relation to others, which informs the mutual behaviors between us and them. Understanding the developments and origins of identity will allow us to move the margins and redefine the center, helping us find inner liberation from our marginality.

To come to understand one's identity, one needs to return to a denied heritage that comes from living between two cultures while not belonging to either one. This will allow one to renew and reimagine one's identity with different starting points and endings.[4] This creative process will aid in creating new selves and new understandings of where we want to find ourselves, which will be liberating and empowering.

The margins in which we exist can become our fighting ground. We reclaim them as our exclusive territory, which those at the center are typically approving of, as they preserve the divisions between the margin and the center. This can occur if the center and the margins retain their power relations. The social struggle appears to look like a Hydra, whose many heads are not confined to one side of any border and seem to redouble if severed. For meaningful change to happen, we need to assert difference and call everything into question. Trinh T. Minh-ha states, "To use marginality as a starting point rather than an ending point is also to cross beyond it towards other affirmations and negations. There cannot be any grand totalizing integration without massive suppression, which is a way of recirculating the effects of domination."[5] Decolonization often means dispelling some of the nonliberative standards and norms. It rarely means dismissing all of them, such as when India retained a large portion of the English culture in its English-speaking civil service and rail lines. Displacing and shifting the center becomes a way of surviving. It is a story of living in between paradigms of truth. Embracing this reality will allow us to reconcile with a shared identity.

Living in the margins means being part of the whole, but pushed outward and outside the main body.[6] It is a revision of Paul's understanding of the body of Christ. But what if the margin consists of the eyes, mouth, hands, or feet—all of them giving meaning, energy, and life to the main body? When the main body ceases to pay attention to its vital parts, it does so to the detriment of itself. Thus, marginality is necessary for the dominant to remain dominating. It indicates that the margin is the centerpiece of the dominant's survival—the blood and fuel of the dominant's supremacy. To be identified as in-between is its own state of radical being, one that allows for innovation and creativity.[7] Shifting our understanding of marginality to something that is necessary for the people in the nonmargins to remain where they are can allow us to repossess our power and our essentiality in wider society.

If we only view the margin as a fence marking the condition of our pain and deprivation, then certain hopelessness will permeate the very core of our being. In collective despair, where the oppressors may also colonize people's minds, one's creativity is at risk, and freedom may be lost. We must resist colonization—work that begins within one's colonized community and family. We need to recognize that margins can be sites of repression and sites of resistance.[8] However, if we fail to resist, we fall silent and ultimately comply. We become resigned in our ways and sit comfortably in our marginality.

Within the margins, the dominant easily marginalize the other, stripping them of their own deserved political power. Prominent feminist writer bell hooks has experienced the reality that those who label themselves radical, critical, and feminist thinkers and participate in constructing a discourse about the other become othered by the dominant writers and academics in their field. Hooks argues that the center and margin separate us into opposing groups. These categories remain if we continue to believe that power derives from a single, central source. Different agencies may mediate power, but the dominance of the central power remains undiminished.[9] Power disburses. The marginalized must recognize that power also exists in the margins.

We can be uplifted by the notion that the margins can also be a place of momentous power. Marginality can be a place of hopelessness or it can be a place of resistance for the oppressed and exploited.[10] Some do not realize that they are marginalized and thus find no reason to resist. However, once we realize that resistance can be empowerment, we recognize that it is crucial to fight. In this fight, we vigorously and peacefully deny the oppression, exploitation, and colonization that has befallen us and our ancestors.

The margin is a place to erase the distinction between the colonized and the colonizer when we see how the margin can become a site of resistance to the center.[11] This site of creativity is a place where we recognize that marginalized voices can be heard and celebrated. Asian American voices have always been seen as secondary. But by recognizing that the space in the margin can be a creative site of resistance, it then becomes a place to reimagine theology. We need to envision new ways of conceiving God in the midst of oppression and marginalization.

When this is all done, then a newer understanding of the divine, the wholly other who is the creator of all beings and loves all creatures, can emerge. We who see ourselves in the margins no longer need to have our laments silenced. Instead, we need to fight whatever forces are holding us in marginal places. The center itself needs to not only move to the margins but avoid defining the margins as well. There can be multiple centers. Then those on the margins will develop new definitions of themselves and establish new relations with those who erase boundaries and join the marginal in one community.[12]

Intersectionality as an Invitation to a Theology of Visibility

Intersectionality is a vital tool to help us reimagine a progressive theology that uncovers and fights against the oppression perpetuated by white European theology. Intersectionality recognizes that people experience multiple intersecting systems of oppression simultaneously. Intersectionality helps us understand how racism, sexism, ethnicity, and patriarchy contribute to the subordination of Asian American women in the theological enterprise.

As discussed in my co-written book, *Intersectional Theology* with Susan Shaw, intersectional analysis moves away from traditional Western theology's use of single-axis thinking and relies on "both/and" as an analytical metric. Intersectionality takes into account the simultaneously experienced social locations, identities, and institutions that shape individual and collective experience within hierarchically structured systems of power and privilege. It is kaleidoscopic, perpetually shifting patterns of power. It is confluent, a point where identities, locations, institutions, and power flow together, creating something new.[13]

As we try to eliminate sexism in the church, we must first recognize how an intersectional measure helps us uncover the multidimensional issues that lead to women's oppression. Korean American women, intersecting both cultures and facing new challenges in a patriarchal Asian culture, are oppressed by not only racism but classism, educational status, gender, cultural history, and religious history as well. There are many dimensions that contribute to women's oppression. At the same time, patriarchy must not be understood solely as male supremacy and sexism but as the multiplicative interweaving of racism, sexism, class exploitation, militarist colonialism, and dehumanizing exclusion, whether it be religious or cultural.[14] Sexism isn't a level playing field but a complex and multifaceted formation. The different issues are key to understanding sexism against women of color, especially Asian American women.

We need to be aware of intersectionality, especially when it comes to understanding Asian American women as intersectional. First, intersectionality approaches lived identities as interlaced and systems of oppression as enmeshed and mutually reinforcing: one aspect of identity or form of inequality is not treated as separable. The various axes of difference work together to cause oppression.[15] For Asian American women, the intersecting axes are Confucian culture, patriarchal Asian history, and racism and sexism in America, which create multiple layers of oppression. An individual's identity is always multidimensional, and sources of oppression and power are as well. Therefore, sexism is not so easily discussed as an issue relegated to gender, as many other aspects must be brought into the conversation to gain a holistic view. Thus, it is necessary to talk about Black women separately from Asian American women, as there are many facets of sexism that different groups of women face that lead directly to their marginality and subordination.

Intersectionality highlights the workings of racist sexism: for instance, intersectionality's matrix model changes the terms of what "counts" as a gender, race, sexuality, disability, ethnicity, or class issue or framework. This concept of interconnectedness also approaches lived identities and systemic patterns of asymmetrical life opportunities and harms from intervening spaces. Intersectional thinking leads to an understanding that what is needed to effect change is to contest shared thinking across systems of domination.[16]

This dynamic interrelatedness is not just about identities; it is also about institutions and systems of power that construct our societies. bell hooks, a Black feminist writer and professor, conveys that feminists should not try to bond over shared experiences of victimization as women or some abstract notion of womanhood; rather, they should bond over a shared political commitment to ending sexist oppression. We need to remember that systems of power and privilege take advantage of women.[17] Intersectionality recognizes how power works across many forms of difference and acknowledges that oppressive powers cannot be isolated or examined separately from one other. Thus, all structures of power, including church structures, need to be reformed to remove oppressive practices. For example, in taking a look at how power is unevenly distributed in the church, we can obviously discern that the Catholic Church still prohibits women from becoming priests, while some Protestant churches do not accept female leadership at all. This is indicative of the patriarchal structure that continues to domineer the church. Such a construction gravely limits the positions of power women are allowed to inhabit, thus controlling how they can contribute. For women of color, the intersection between gender and race in the church can lead to the other challenge of compounded marginalization and lack of visibility. For Asian American women, this common yet silent narrative of othering and oppression must be eliminated.

We must use an intersectional lens to fully understand how patriarchy and sexism work to subordinate Asian American women. As a part of what Patricia Hill Collins calls "the matrix of domination," that place where intersecting social identities and institutions of power overlap, theology plays a role in maintaining hierarchies.[18] Thus, intersectional thinking is a praxis for theology that is extremely helpful in locating and reforming structures of power. Intersectionality is not simply a way of theorizing; it is a method for identifying actions. Intersectional thinking restores an activist center to our theology, demanding that what we think remains connected to what we do; it asserts the ultimate priority of engagement with the world. The end goal of theological thought and discussion must be to reach for positive social change for the most marginalized. Theology is never removed from the real lives of human beings and their suffering. It is never something that ends with ideas; it should always translate into action.

As I have contended with Susan Shaw, intersectional theology begins in the intersections of one's multiple identities and moves toward justice for all people.[19] As a praxis, theology calls for resistance and activism within a global context. It considers how different bodies exist in different landscapes, and it calls for a close analysis of ever-changing social, economic, political, and religious realities to create nimble theologies that drive the work of liberation. Doing intersectional theology demands that we are attuned to current politics and existing culture, calling on us to continually engage with, protest against, and connect with the world around us. Since politics and theology should never be removed from people's lives, we must study and comprehend the institutions and systems of power alongside a quickly evolving culture that grapples with the minimization, subjugation, and erasure of Asian American women.

Intersectional Humanity Made Visible in Jesus

As I grew up in the church in Canada, I searched for my human value in light of the abundant sexism and racism I experienced. Why was I being tested by this isolation? How could I use these experiences, these wounds, to protect and educate other Asian Americans? As I searched for answers, I wondered who Jesus was and how Jesus understood our value as God's children.

Jesus gives us many examples of what it means to be human, but most simply, Jesus shows us that to be human is to be connected to others—to love our neighbors and our enemies and to love God. When we think about marginalized people, we must heed their powerlessness and give back their deserved agency.

Jesus embodies justice through example, not dogma. Not by lording it over others but by serving them, by hearing the word of God and doing it (Luke 8:19–21). Jesus wants reconciliation of divided peoples over worship. It is through relating to others—the poor, the sick, and the outcast—that Jesus reveals himself as the liberator, reconciler, and healer, exhibiting to us not only how to be human but the value of being human.[20] That is why we also seek the margins and places of invisibility to see how we can find God and apply God's lessons. God is present among the invisible peoples who are seeking new ways of being in Jesus's gospel.

Jesus the liberator and compassionate leader inaugurated the kin-dom of God by proclaiming the kin-dom rather than himself. The kin-dom of God is already but not yet, the reality that has already begun but will not be fulfilled until the end time.[21] Jesus opens the expanse of the kin-dom of God by relating with and showing a preference for the sinners, the outcasts, the marginalized, the poor, and the powerless.[22] But our society tends to do the opposite. In a culture of celebrity news and following, we often turn to the rich and powerful for guidance in our lives. We want the strong to give us their power. Hence our lives become a pursuit of earthly riches, and we neglect the marginalized whom Jesus commanded us to embrace and live selflessly for.

Jesus was born of a simple Jewish woman. He was not born into anything but an ordinary family, representing the poor, oppressed, marginalized, and exploited people of his time. His ministry was to proclaim the good news to the poor, "liberty to captives, sight to the blind, [and] to let the oppressed go free" (Luke 4:18). Jesus was radical in how he associated with the lower classes, the oppressed, the invisible, and the foreigners.[23] The lepers were the most marginalized of that society—they were outcasts, shunned by everyone because of the disease—but Jesus met lepers and cured them. In the New Testament, Jesus cures ten lepers (Luke 17:15–19) whom society rejected. Simon, the leper, hosts Jesus when Mary anoints Jesus's feet.

Jesus was moved by the Syrophenician woman of Canaanite ancestry who exhibited great faith (Matt 15:21–28). Rather than ignore her and listen to his disciples, who urged him to send her away, Jesus engages her in conversation. Jesus tells her, "I was sent only to the lost sheep of the house of Israel" (15:24). She challenges Jesus, and as a result, Jesus surprisingly grants her request (15:28). Jesus sees those who are pushed to the side and empathizes with them. Through embracing them, he brings them forward and above.

There are other gospel stories of Jesus welcoming those who have been made invisible by wider society. Jesus tells a story of the good Samaritan whose actions epitomize how one should act toward one's neighbor in distress (Luke 10:29–37) to show how we are all to act toward those in the margins. The good Samaritan, who himself is marginalized within that society, does what those who are in the center fail to do: he takes care of the man who was robbed and beaten and left on the side of the road.

There is also the story of the strong faith of the centurion and his concern for his ill servant (Luke 7:1–10). The servant is a part of Roman society who, not being an officer or even a legionnaire, does not have much freedom or agency. Jesus could have easily ignored the servant, but instead, he makes the servant well. Jesus cared for the marginalized and those who were often ignored by Jewish society. As Jesus reaches out and welcomes those who are cast aside, he shows us how we are to be human.[24]

Christians base human dignity on the notion that God made people in God's image and likeness. The word *person* comes from the Latin word *persona*, which means "an actor's mask." In certain ways, God is present here on earth with a "mask" of a person or as an avatar in the form of a person. Thus, the person may be the clearest reflection of God among us who loves us and embraces the marginalized and invisible in our society. We are to respect the sacredness of the human being because a person is what we know of God in our daily lives and encounters. If Christians believe that God made us in God's image, then to ridicule, racialize, and make someone invisible for the way God created them is, in effect, to ridicule God as a creator who made us the way we are to be.[25]

Being created in the image of God provides a vision for humanity toward which we can live and work—focused on Jesus as our model for living (in the way of Jesus). As previously mentioned, Jesus reached out to the lepers. They were placed outside the city and told to live among themselves. There was no six-foot rule or disposable paper masks. The same sorts of things happened in Korea. Korean lepers were put in an isolated colony. Society exempted those with disabled bodies, those who had the most to gain from the help of others. The lepers become important to Jesus. Jesus doesn't neglect them but listens to them and heals them. These acts restore the lepers' humanity, a pursuit Jesus personifies as a person from an oppressed group of people. Jesus is for those who are ostracized, cast out, and invisible.

We are reconciled through God. God has embraced the world in Jesus Christ—forgiving and liberating us from sin—making us new creations. This enables us to live by faith—as countercultural people who live in peace, love, and justice toward others. We need to work faithfully to reconcile with one another. This action of reconciliation gives us hope as we fight against invisibility, dehumanization, and the structural powers aligned against us. We understand that we are not alone in this marginalization but continue to live in hope, faith, and love.

Invisibility of Women in the Bible

Taking a look at our world today, we find that while the profile of Asian Americans may rise in the popular American imagination, the Asian American woman is still shrouded in obscurations created by the white dominant society. The visible and invisible in society are reflected throughout Scripture as a major biblical theme.

Sociologically, most women have been invisible throughout history, but Asian American women's invisibility contrasts with the growing prominence of white feminists—white women who are often aligned with the model minority Asian American women. Invisibility may mean powerlessness, voicelessness, marginality, and an inability to put forward unique issues. Therefore, it is important to reimagine the dominant theology into a fully progressive, inclusive, and intersectional praxis that can lead to the awareness, understanding, and acceptance of our Asian neighbors and prevent the silencing of the voices of Asian American women.

Understanding how Jesus sought to counter biblical women's invisibility helps us better practice a theology of visibility that empowers Asian American women. We see it in stories about foreign women, lepers, the Samaritan woman, and Mary Magdalene. The roles of women in the Bible are believed to have been not presented in full or omitted entirely during and after the Bible was written. Even when women are present in the stories, their names are usually not given. We have the woman who anointed Jesus's feet (Luke 7:36–50), Lot's wife (Gen 19:15–26), Jephthah's daughter (Judges 11), the woman caught in adultery (John 8:1–11), the Samaritan woman at the well (John 4:4–26), the poor yet generous widow (Luke 21:1–4), the Canaanite woman (Matt 15:21–28), and the bleeding woman (Matt 9:20–22). The exclusion of these women's names marginalizes them and further makes them invisible.

The stories of no-name women in the Bible provide some insight into why women were made invisible during biblical times as well as throughout much of church history. Asian American women are seen as a moral threat, defined by the image of being a subservient, hypersexualized lure to white men. Therefore, dominant society created the Asian American as invisible, silent, and unnamed.

In Luke's Gospel, the story of the sinful woman shows how patriarchy attempts to erase women's presence, while God intends to lift women up (Luke 7:36–50). Sin for biblical women was often associated with sex, leading some to infer that the women were prostitutes. In this story, an anonymous woman comes into the Pharisee's house and anoints Jesus. The no-name woman learns that Jesus is eating at the Pharisee's house, so she enters with an expensive alabaster jar of perfume. She stands behind Jesus, weeping, and her tears began to wet Jesus's feet. She then wipes his feet with her hair, kisses them, and pours perfume on them. Jesus creates a lesson of love and forgiveness from this event. It becomes an important lesson, as it exemplifies Jesus's incarnation, ministry, crucifixion, and resurrection.

However, the woman's identity and name are not given. Only her "sinful" character is remembered and written in the Scriptures regarding her identity. The male biblical writer wanted to emphasize that the woman was probably a prostitute. The way this story is written reveals how patriarchy tries to highlight the sin of women and not patriarchy, which oftentimes forces vulnerable young women to become sex slaves or prostitutes. Patriarchal writers eliminate women from historical events, as women's names were less important in society. Women are viewed in relation to men, as this woman is described as "sinful" in the sense that her sin is tied to her sexuality. Despite the beauty of the symbolic preparation for the upcoming burial of Jesus, this event will forever be tied to her sexual "sin."

When God created the world, God made men and women equally. Men and women were intended to be the exemplars of creation loving and caring for the other, not dominating the other. Creation was beautiful, and everything in it was good. We must not continuously portray women as evil; they are good, essential, valuable, and chosen by God. Though the biblical women discussed here are remembered despite their ambiguity, they have no names and no faces—they are invisible.

The Costs of Invisibility

What happens to the invisible? Not only are they not seen by the dominant society, but their voices are also drowned out or ignored. The loss of Asian American women's individual and communal voice is a detriment to society, as their voices can fuel social and cultural change.

When I think about my own Asian heritage, I see that many Asian American voices are pushed to the margins and made invisible. Their cries of racism, discrimination, and stereotyping get muffled through the "model minority myth" or the bestowing of the title "honorary whites." These terms are used to downplay Asian Americans' suffering. Because of this forced invisibility, Asian Americans lack social, political, and cultural power. Therefore, embracing a theology of visibility will take us one step closer to eliminating the evils of racism, discrimination, sexism, and xenophobia that continue to oppress Asian American women.

Asian American Women Contributing to a Theology of Visibility

The voices of Asian American women are powerful. They add the richness of Asian philosophy, religion, and culture. They add a new, liberative dimension to a white heteronormative theology by integrating Asian heritage, practices, and beliefs. Asian American women have the power to diversify the human spectrum of Christian identities and uplift the voices of all other marginalized women. As Asian American women work toward a theology of visibility, they should seek to empower other oppressed, invisible groups to move beyond their experiences of discrimination and claim their space in the kin-dom of God.

My Asian identity has greatly informed my understanding of God and visibility within my spiritual journey. There are four Korean concepts that shed light on how the Holy Spirit improvises a praxis of visibility.[26] These four elements help Asian American women live in a theology of visibility that draws them away from the shadowed fringes, brings the invisible others out into the light, and embraces them all in the center.

Those who practice a theology of visibility should feel enriched and blessed with the education that heritage provides. Asian Americans are endowed with complex culture, abundant in ideas and concepts that challenge and complement those from the West. The deep, collective sense of the Asian experience comes from the concept of *ou-ri*, meaning "our," as well as the concepts of *han*, which can be translated as "unjust suffering"; *jeong*, which means "sticky love"; and Chi, an Asian concept that signifies the spirit. These concepts help define Asian society by organizing the collective sense of self and shared group identity, which contradict the ideals of Western society. For Asian American women to become visible as full participants in the kin-dom of God, theology must embrace these Asian concepts and make them part of the theological conversation. In many ways, this discussion recaptures the remarkable boundary crossing that characterized the early church.[27]

Ou-ri

Community overrides individualism in Asian society. Such a standard is imbued directly into the language of Asian societies, shifting the manner of our perception of the world and the identities it holds. The Korean language encompasses words signifying the community over the self, the family over the individual. For instance, *ou-ri*, a possessive plural, means "our." In Korea, the possessive noun *my* is seldom used; instead, we use the plural possessive noun *our*. We say not "my mother" but rather "our mother," even in families with just one child, as there is a sense of community or a larger family. The Korean family structure is delineated with the uncles on the father's side being called "big father" if older or "younger father" if younger. Their wives are correspondingly called "big mother" or "younger mother." The "mother" language used to identify the wife of the uncle signifies that the extended patriarchal family is still key to the survival of the nuclear family. Plural possessive pronouns are also used for other possessions, such as "our house," not "my house." Even when you are referring to your own spouse, you say not "my spouse" but "our spouse" even though you are only married to one person.[28]

The use of the plural possessive noun may seem like a small and insignificant factor in how one does theology, but it does change things. Using the plural possessive noun like it is used in Korea, even for singular possessives, will alter how one views oneself, others, creation, and God. The plural possessive moves us away from focusing on our individual selves and toward the greater collective. It forces us to look at community, the body of Christ, and the communion of saints as elemental forces that exist harmoniously outside Western individualism. Taking on a widened perspective, the Korean concept of plural possessive nouns pushes us to consider not only ourselves, care not only for ourselves, regard not only ourselves but the larger community and all of creation.

Words are all we have in theology. Words shape our minds, our ideas, and even our histories, painting our past and future with transient associations and understandings. For example, in the United States, we call a particular conflict the Vietnam War, but in Vietnam, they call it the American War. Language here makes a big difference, changing how we recognize a war that raged for nineteen years, from 1955 to 1975, with major US involvement beginning around 1964. This example can be paralleled with what Americans call Columbus Day, a commemoration of Christopher Columbus's landing in the Americas in 1492. However, this is only the beginning of Western European colonialization, as five hundred years before Columbus, Vikings led by Leif Erikson settled in the United States, and some scholars argue that Chinese explorers came even before that. But the original people are the Native Americans. As a consequence, to have an honest title for the founding people of this land, Columbus Day should be replaced with Native American Day or Indigenous Peoples' Day.

When we turn to theology, the use of possessive plural "our God" rather than the singular possessive "my God" shifts the paradigm of viewing Christianity on an individual level to a community level. The Lord's Prayer actually says, "Our Father, who art in heaven" and not "My God, who art in heaven," with *our* reinforcing the idea of a communal prayer rather than an individual prayer to God. It emphasizes the importance of community over the individual.

Trinitarian language offers a communal rather than an individualistic perspective of God. The three-in-oneness of God, or the Trinity, shows us how we are to be in communion with one another. The Christian community and collectiveness should ultimately push us to care for the other, especially the poor, the marginalized, and the invisible people whom Christ loved and embraced. Christianity is a religion not about "me" but about "us"—one that prioritizes the inclusion and care of all peoples. To its own detriment, Western Christianity has been heavily influenced by dualism, a philosophy that can be traced to Aristotle's writings. Dualism dismantles concepts down into polarized identities. For example, heaven and earth, man and woman, spirit and body, and so on. In the East, how we view the world is influenced not by dualism but rather by an approach characterized as being "both/and." One can be both spirit and matter, and heaven is earth.

The nondualistic Eastern way of thinking changes our perspective of the world and of ourselves as it moves us to become a more inclusive and less separated and divided world. As a result, *ou-ri* dominates our psyche and behavior. When Koreans use the plural possessive noun *our* even for singular possession, it changes how we view ourselves, our family, our neighbors, and others. It reveals that what seems to be and often feels like a singularly traveled life is actually an interconnected one—a life that cannot be survived as an island alone but rather demands the nurturing and cultivation of community. Furthermore, living in a culture of *ou-ri* alters our perspective of God.

Thus, we must ask ourselves, Does the church exist to help us develop in Christ as an individual, or has God tasked us with helping the church develop both qualitatively and quantitatively? Though the answer is yes to both, of course, it is important to consider that a partial collective approach to our Christianity—much like early Christians who prioritized the nature and health of God's community over the objectives of individual believers—can be beneficial for Asian American women seeking to live a theology of visibility. We do so by recognizing God's vision of a creation that exists to reinforce the lives of others, calling on us to strengthen the community, a prerequisite to strengthening our individual faith.

The Bible says, "The glory that you have given me I have given them, so that they may be one, *as we are one*, I in them and you in me, that they may become completely one, so that the world may know that you have sent me and have loved them even as you have loved me" (John 17:22–23; emphasis added). Take note of the astounding italicized phrase. Here, Jesus prays that his followers will experience the same standard of interpersonal relationships that he experiences with God the Father. What cultural orientation best upholds Jesus's vision? The "strong-group" church or the "me-and-Jesus" perspective that marks Western Christianity today? I believe that the former should not be dismissed as a cultural alternative that is unfit for contemporary churches today, as it is based on the foundation of the very nature of our Trinitarian God, who is in community with the Father, Son, and the Holy Spirit. The three persons are relational. The individuality of the West overshadows the communal activity of the Trinity, but the East reminds us of its importance in our theological journey. We also should not forget this idea being affirmed by Jesus when he regards his disciples as family (Mark 3:31–35). The Trinitarian God wants to be in communion with creation. As we relate to God with all of creation, we recognize a panentheistic God in all creation.[29]

The Korean word *ou-ri* focuses on community and how each person is important. *Ou-ri* can help Asian American women live in a theology of visibility that draws them from the shadows and brings others in congruent positions of invisibility out into the light, beaming toward the center. Yet despite the binary that exists between the core cultural aspects of the West and East, individualism and collectivism, we should take solace in the knowledge that they are not mutually exclusive. Within any given cultural environment, it is simply a matter of emphasis.

Like us, early Christians exercised their volition and made choices as individuals. Unlike us, however, early Christians made these choices not in the service of personal goals or desires but for the good of the group, the shared family of God.

As evidenced, the biblical worldview privileges the group over the individual. Nevertheless, Scripture does not commend a sense of blind group loyalty devoid of singularized identity and personal autonomy. Overemphasizing group loyalty and solidarity to the exclusion of individual rights and desires produces its own set of issues. There remains a space in the Christian worldview for what we might call a sanctified individualism.[30]

So then how does this coincide with a collectivist Christian community view in which the welfare of the church is privileged over one's personal relationship with God? Quite well, actually. For God had called Abraham not to be an isolated pilgrim of spiritual self-actualization but to be the father of a nation. Jesus also challenged his disciples to make significant countercultural choices as individuals, choices that would profoundly affect their lives (Mark 1:16–20; 10:17–30; Matt 8:21–22). In every case, the decision was not a choice for *in*dependence; it was a decision for *inter*dependence.

To return to language, *ou-ri* reveals that we are all interdependent on one another. We cannot survive on an island by ourselves but need the community that nurtures us and gives us life. Strong-group Christianity transcends the boundaries of culture and time. And it flies in the face of the individualistic, often consumerist approach to the church as an institution that has captivated the hearts of so many in America today.

Han

Koreans have a word to express painful suffering, described as a piercing of the heart. This type of pain comes from unjust misery. When there are systems set up to cause suffering, then *han* is experienced. *Han* is caused by racism, colonialism, slavery, and sexism, which establish the subordination, exploitation, and oppression of groups of people. The suffering is amplified by the gravity of the circumstances and the feeling of being unable to escape the systems that cause the suffering.

Han causes a wound in one's heart, and if one cannot find a source of healing, it is believed that the pain is carried on to death or is the cause of one's death. In this way, *han* can be passed from one generation to the next. Unresolved feelings of sorrow, grief, and suffering can linger on for decades, affecting the victim's children and their children. *Han* can be experienced individually or collectively—for example, Native Americans and European Jews suffering from genocide and Africans suffering from American slavery. Koreans have experienced communal *han* from the oppressive era of Japanese imperialism, when Koreans lost their Korean names, culture, language, society, and religion.

Han forces us to recognize the pain and suffering that occurs as a result of evil human constructs. It reminds us that sin isn't just a vertical event against God; it is also a horizontal one against our neighbors. Theology needs to deal with the circumstances that cause us to sin against others and work toward some form of liberation from the devastating pain of *han*. Asian American women are wounded due to racism, discrimination, patriarchy, and sexism from both white society and Asian American culture. Their experience of oppression goes deep and is carried on to their children and grandchildren. They are full of *han*, and this experience reminds them of the need for a theology of visibility that can decenter white male Euro-theology and lift them out of their pain and suffering.

Jeong

Jeong permeates the lives of Koreans; it is part of what gives joy and meaning to many people's lives. *Jeong* is a difficult word to translate into English, but it can be understood simply as love. However, the term *jeong* encompasses a meaning that is greater and vaster than love, including affection, attachment, compassion, kindness, sharing, connection, and sympathy toward people and objects.

Jeong captures the essence of love and affection between people that is *sticky*, like honey on our fingertips. This sticky kind of love is difficult to separate or untangle oneself from and makes us stay connected to one another. Even though you may argue or fight with your friend, spouse, or family member, *jeong* will bring you back together. *Jeong* flows out of you to the other, causing you both to feel connectedness, affection, and love. There is no logical reason or validation for why one experiences *jeong*; it just happens.[31] It is a positive experience that emphasizes how we need one another for survival, as we are social beings who require connection in order to thrive.

Jeong is located within one's heart and between individuals. This feeling between individuals is similar to the Eastern notion of collective emotion and the deep-rooted sense of community. There is also a sense of collectiveness or community, as *jeong* diminishes the "I" and the boundaries attached to it and blurs the distinctions between people.[32] The experience of collectiveness is common in Asia, which keeps people accountable to one another. It is largely absent in the Western world but could be something westerners accept and enact, rather than the usual comparative acknowledgment, and even learn from.

Jeong is understood as a bond between people. It is a love that keeps people together even in the midst of pain and suffering. It often feels like the unconditional bond between friends and family that is not dependent on one's actions but present because of the relationship that exists. *Jeong* can be tied into the concept of the Spirit that reminds us of our connectedness to one another, to the Spirit, and to God. We cannot live alone; we require *jeong* to help us form feelings of love and being loved. Furthermore, we cannot separate ourselves from God, as God is within us and among us. It is the Spirit of God that draws us to live in peace with one another, encourages us to love our neighbor, and provokes us to reach out in love to others.[33]

Jeong is pervasive not just within Korean culture but also within many other collectivist Asian cultures. It is an intangible yet unbreakable bond that keeps families, friends, and coworkers together even despite hardship or turmoil. A theology of visibility should build people up to allow *jeong* to anchor communities, churches, families, and friends together to endure any and all adversity. *Jeong*, as part of a theology of visibility, is a framework that maintains loyalty, devotion, and love between people and their communities—particularly those who have been disenfranchised and separated. A theology of visibility works to illuminate discriminatory acts of violence, xenophobia, sexism, and so on that target people of color, especially Asian American women. As this ongoing history of intolerance is exposed, a theology of visibility can be practiced to uplift Asian American women who have been marginalized and made invisible by white society. *Jeong*, a sticky love, will help build up communities and help them live into the kin-dom of God. Oftentimes, we philosophize God's love for us, and it all appears abstract. *Jeong* makes love concrete and actualized. We recognize that no one should be cast away or made invisible; all must be brought into the kin-dom of God.

Chi

Spirit, or the Holy Spirit, is expressed in more than one language in the Bible—in Hebrew in the Old Testament as *ruach* and in Greek as *pneuma* in the New Testament. As theology becomes global, our language must evolve to integrate words from other cultures. These other languages and ways of life are crucial to expanding our understanding of God and move us toward a universal theological discourse. Asians make up 60 percent of the world's population. This is important to keep in mind as Christianity spreads and becomes more popular in Asia and less popular in Europe and North America. It is past time to use Asian words and concepts in Christian theology to help us all get a better understanding of the mystery of the divine.

Chi is an Asian concept similar to the biblical words *ruach* and *pneuma*. The word *Chi* means "wind," "energy," and "breath," but it gives a more embodied sense of the Spirit, which is sometimes lost in contemporary Western understandings of "spirit." In the Western world, the body tends to be seen as separate from Spirit, and in white Eurocentric Christianity, the Holy Spirit is sometimes portrayed as a disembodied, abstract concept.[34] Chi helps us understand that the Spirit lives in us and is a part of our selves.[35]

Christian theologians should start using *Chi* in the same ways that they use *ruach* and *pneuma*. Theologians should not self-select and limit their languages but use languages and words that are helpful from any culture. The Asian concept of Chi is a more inclusive and powerful way of speaking about God. It makes visible Asian American women who have otherwise been made invisible by white American society.

To lift people up, especially Asian American women, it becomes crucial to study, embrace, and utilize the oppressed culture's words and concepts to help expand the theological discourse and imagination and become inclusive of Asian American women. This will not destroy Christianity; it will strengthen it. Christians, in their finiteness, worship an infinite God. We can never fully understand the infinite God, and therefore, we need to use as many words and concepts as we can to expand our understandings and experiences.

Chi is within our bodies; it is the life-giving Spirit that is part of our daily tasks. When we die, Chi leaves our bodies and makes us cold. In Korea, we sometimes greet one another with "How is your Chi?" We aim to recognize the Chi of our neighbors and loved ones and whether one's Chi is low or high. It is through the everyday experience of the Spirit in our lives, and not just a Sunday worship experience, that one comes to understand the Holy Spirit.[36] In the written Chinese language, there is a distinction made among heavenly, earthly, and human Chi, but they are essentially the same Chi that moves around and gives life to all things. In my own theological writing, I don't differentiate the three written forms of Chi, just as I don't differentiate the Spirit of God from the Spirit that is within us and all living things.

In the West, we are familiar with tae kwon do, tai chi, and Reiki, which physically and psychologically address the concept of Chi. In a tae kwon do class, the grand master will ask the students to harness their Chi as they practice their movements. Reiki is a form of healing that uses the energy, or Chi, from one's hands to help bring healing to others. Tai chi involves getting in tune with the spirit in the body to help us move and bring healing to our bodies. Chi is a spirit that envelopes all of life. It is a panentheistic view of heavenly Chi being interrelated and integrated with the world in God and God being in the world just as the Holy Spirit is. In theology of visibility, it is important to see how Chi deepens and widens our understanding of the Holy Spirit through energy and movement as it reminds us of the lived experiences of the Spirit in everyday life.[37] Chi is in all living things, and Chi will strengthen Asian American women in their full humanity and empower them to be liberated and strong.

To fall into dualistic thinking as a Christian is a pitfall. It incites the idea that matter and spirit are separate. We see this in our Christian practice—for example, the body is evil and the spirit is good, male is good and female is evil. The divide is clear and distinct, aiding misguided Christians to categorize the world in absolutes. This kind of thinking falsely justifies male superiority, homophobia, racism, and other expressions of prejudice. What Chi attempts to do is to reveal to us the inevitable, hazy in-between, the unification and interdependence of spirit and matter. Spirit is matter, and the two cannot be separate.

As Chi continues to remind us of the togetherness of these separate realms, it leads us to visibility. This is the theology of visibility. By making known how people such as Asian American women are oppressed, marginalized, and pushed aside, a theology of visibility can innovate our understanding of God through the advocacy for the invisible and the pursuit of liberation. A theology of visibility places an emblazoned, clarifying lens over our eyes, allowing us to finally see and uplift those we have not seen in society—those who are often part of our own community. As Asian American women practice this theology, they gradually gain collective, increased visibility through a network of shared empowerment, conspicuity, and agency. The new way of understanding God is to understand God as Chi who is within us and strives to heal the brokenness within, or *han*. Chi tries to build up Asian American women as well as the Asian American community so that they can stand in solidarity in the midst of racism, subordination, and xenophobia. Theology of visibility is an attempt at seeing anew—seeing with eyes that can finally embrace the fullness of God, the breath of the divine that is within all of us.

As Chi is an Asian concept similar to the biblical words *ruach* and *pneuma*, we can easily contextualize this idea in the Western theological space. Chi can be embraced as an inclusionary method of speaking about the Spirit of God. It offers Asian American listeners a parallel, a transcendental idea with which they are already acquainted in Asian culture, to give meaning to the enigma of the Spirit. Asian American women can then share the meaning of the Spirit with other women in their community, thereby giving them religious visibility, granting them the opportunity to grow closer with God.

Eastern ways of understanding Spirit as an embodied Spirit take us away from the dualistic patterns of thinking that simplify our perception of the divine and can enable us to envision a more complex, less crystallized Spirit—one that is the body and a body that is the Spirit. Dualism clearly separates the body from the Spirit, whereas Asian concepts and understanding do not divide but lead us to understand that they are intertwined and together. With this holistic approach, we can begin to embrace a stronger theology—one that helps us open our eyes and see the problems of white, Eurocentric, male-dominated doctrine and redirects us toward a theology of embracing all people in their full complexity and contradictions. As Chi seeks bodies, a theology of visibility welcomes the Chi-filled body, Asian American women's bodies, and makes them more visible and full of life, energy, love, and power. It is important to accept Asian words and ideas to create a universal discourse. Just as European theologians used German words such as gemeinschaft (community) and *Geist* (spirit), Asian terms can imbue Christian ideas with the profundity of historic Eastern thought and philosophies that shape not just how Eastern societies operate today but how our world culture develops in the current whirl of globalization and migration. Asian concepts of Chi, *ou-ri, jeong*, and *han* move us toward a theology of visibility that is empowering, enlightening, and liberating.

These Asian conceptions can make positive contributions to our theological reimagining and reformulating in America, as they try to dismantle the structures of racism, xenophobia, and sexism that have oppressed Asian American women. Those who have attempted to include these Asian concepts have encountered intersectional barriers to such a movement of the Holy Spirit. These barriers are stitched together into a dangerous quilt that continues to smother these new fires of the kin-dom of God. White Eurocentric male theology has its own dangerous tenets that serve to justify forms of discrimination. Naming clearly this barrier to the visible signs of God's kindom is a crucial step toward living into a theology of visibility.

Visibility in the Kin-dom of God

Invisibility has no place in the kin-dom of God, which embraces all people and values each person. The kin-dom of God does not erase people's names or eliminate groups of people. Rather, it is a large banquet where all are welcome to the feast set before us by God.

We are all created in the image of God. This is part of the invisibility equation. Asian American women bear the image of God, yet they continue to be marginalized, subjugated, oppressed, and made invisible by the church. The church has made a distinction between white men and white women throughout its two-thousand-year history and made women subordinate.[38] However, with the rise of feminist liberation theology in the 1960s, interest in female empowerment began to grow. Even so, Asian American women and other women of color were seldom included in this social change, as they were held back by their cultural communities and patriarchy.

Invisibility as a theological concept needs to be explored to understand how the marginalized and outcasts should be welcomed into the kin-dom of God. Invisibility is a spiritual issue. It affects how we view and understand God and God's creation and how we treat one another in this global world. Asian American voices are subject to compounded marginalization within the social and theological world.

Today, we are reminded as Asian Americans that we matter. Our voices matter, and our presence matters. We bear the image of God in the unique way that only we can. Asian American women who bear the image of Christ should be celebrated within the kin-dom of God. An invisible God to humanity rejoices in the diversity of God's creation, and Asian American women add richness to the beautiful diversity of God's creation and kin-dom.

Explorations in a Theology of Visibility

In the present moment, we have the opportunity to rebuild a theology that addresses the invisibility experienced by Asian Americans, particularly Asian American women who are made invisible in the family, church, and wider society. Intersectional theology reminds us to take into consideration race, ethnicity, gender, sexuality, ableism, education, and so on in understanding how we do theology. Asian American women also need to evaluate how others view them, as these perceptions have an impact on how they interact in society and understand themselves. Asian American women need to reflect on their invisibility and how they can move toward a life of political, social, and spiritual visibility, agency, and empowerment.

Asian American women are created by God and share in full dignity and value as God's children. This gives hope for liberation and visibility because it means there is genuine connectedness and mutuality among all people. The true humanity God intends is found in Jesus Christ. This empowers us by showing us that we can live open and inclusive lives toward all people—in the ways we treat them and how they treat us. Asian American women as countercultural people want to live in peace, love, and justice toward others. God's Spirit is with them as they seek to overcome the invisibility that dehumanizes them. The fullness of God's reign is here and now, since this is God's world, and we are part of God's reign. As discussed previously, we see Jesus providing hope to the invisible by healing the lepers, empowering Mary Magdalene, and healing the hemorrhaging woman. By the power of the Spirit of God, invisible people can be granted the agency to gain power and hope.

It does not matter where we are from or how we orient ourselves; we are all created in the image of God. This means that we are all beautiful and made in the fullness of God—a creator God who loves diversity and relishes how each created person is so different from the other. God's creation is diverse, and this makes it all so beautiful. We are all connected and reliant on one another. We need each other to survive and thrive. We are created as social beings who are dependent on the other and our communities to bring fullness to our lives.

Conclusion

The opportunity to write and speak publicly about the aspirations, barriers, and insights that have shaped me has been provocative for me and, I pray, for you. Understanding the theological implications of invisibility is crucial. The invisible God the creator became a human being and became visible through the incarnation. A God whom we can visibly see is a much more commanding God whom we can reference and accept into our lives. The visible God becomes a God whose presence takes over our lives. A visible God gives us assurance of our freedom and love. The visible God makes us all visible. This happens because we are all created in the image of the one infinite God. Thus, we need to view all people as equals.

If we take a closer look at each other, we can see the hidden God becoming visible in us. The Spirit of God is breath. That breath is what keeps us alive. That breath is right in front of you. It is within you. The breath you are taking in is God. Therefore, since all are breathing, we cannot monopolize the Spirit of God and say that God is only present within the church or that God is present only in the Eurocentric church. God's Spirit is in all people. Therefore, it prompts us to acknowledge the racism, sexism, xenophobia, and discrimination that individuals, society, and the church participate in. We must repent against these wrongs in the journey to self-renewal.

A new self, a new humanity can move toward gaining a closer look into the mystery of the hidden and invisible God. God's reign is happening here and now. God, who is hidden and invisible, is always with us in different ways. God's presence in our lives makes us full, vibrant, and total. The reign of God never ceases; the reign of God defines our today. This empowers us, since we believe in a certain eschatology, and our destination in God's reign reaches out for us now, in the present. This gives us hope that there is a sure end toward which we are moving in the world as we walk in the way of Jesus and work for God's purposes. The meaning of visibility and invisibility in relation to our spirituality can help Asian American women move toward a theology that liberates, uplifts, and empowers. It is an invitation to work toward making Asian American women and others in American society who are marginalized and made invisible feel welcome to the table and to the divine kin-dom of God.

CONCLUSION

My life, accented by passing periods of invisibility and silence, led me down the path to writing this book. For the length of my career, I wondered why, with all our cultural distinction and capital, Asian Americans have been obscured in American society. With the lack of acceptance in a new land, Asians have strived to make their lives known, understood, and celebrated. There has been an increase of Asian immigrants with the passage of the 1965 Immigration and Nationality Act, with the largest groups of immigrants coming to the United States from China, India, and the Philippines.[1] Asian immigrants are the fastest-growing population in the United States, comprising 6 percent of the total population, which is projected to grow to 10 percent by 2050. Thus, recently, Asian Americans have become a more familiar figment of the popular white American imagination. Their characterization, however, lacks the full dimensions of nuance and understanding.

A history laden with exploitation, discrimination, and trivialization created the cliché of the meek, socially awkward, studious, apolitical Asian American whose lone pursuit of bringing honor to their family trumps their quest for meaningful self-fulfillment. For too long, the Asian American was understood as an emblem of self-sacrifice rather than a symbol of radical innovation and adaptability. In addition, Asian Americans were made invisible in a culture that tried to eliminate their experiences of racism and discrimination. Asian American women suffered the prejudices of racism in a white dominant society and sexism found in both the dominant white and Asian American cultures. Such a misunderstanding of Asian Americans and their struggles of invisibility were leading factors in my writing of this book, but perhaps more important was the need to confront the Asian American's relative internalization of the dominant culture's perception of them.

When Asian Americans are told enough times that we are passive, obedient, and marginal, we reach a moment of unconscious assimilation to such perceptions. As we are sidelined and repressed into vague figures of social insignificance, we begin to see such representations as a reflection rather than an impression. These kinds of suggestions led me to uncover the widespread melancholy of Asian Americans—first, second, and third generation—whose melancholy is due not just to our experiences of racism but to the loss of our racial identity. We struggle with in-betweenness, foreignness, and invisibility. As a result, our self-perception oscillates in confusion, often settling into a state of vagueness. As a result, we feel shame and insecurity, which are rooted in the dislocations of immigration and assimilation—in our lack of ability to specifically recognize what we have lost.

Thus, we look into ourselves, our minds, our spirits, and find another place for us to repair the broken ideas we have of ourselves. Coming to God gives us the clarity we need to rewrite and retell our stories.

"American Christianity"

Theology is autobiographical. We come to know God from our experiences. As we reflect on God from our particular circumstances, we must consider multiple practical and cultural contexts.[2]

Asian American women's experiences are valid and important. We need to acknowledge, ponder, and explore them to find God in them.

Furthermore, we need to see how our understanding of God changes our actions and how we ought to live. God is infinite; we are finite beings. We can never come to a full comprehension of God through the finite human mind. However, we should not be discouraged; we must attempt to gain some awareness of God in our lives, remembering that the Christian faith is "faith seeking understanding."[3]

Knowing ourselves and our culture is important to our realization of God. We experience God in and through our cultural, racial, and ethnic contexts. Recognizing race has a different dynamic because of its roots in the experience of exploitation, power, and privilege, but our notions of race and God are interrelated.

In America, we live under the illusion of equality and meritocracy. Schoolchildren recite the Pledge of Allegiance every morning. The pledge ends with the sentiment, "With liberty and justice for all," but the reality of American life reveals that only a portion of the country enjoys true liberty and justice. Often, people of color are not a part of this liberated portion, and Asian American women are not only oppressed but also made invisible.

White American Christians have used God as the author of American exceptionalism, justifying whites as God's chosen race of people. It is no longer Christianity but "Americanity." This is achieved by glorifying and legitimizing atrocities committed against Indians, Blacks, Latinxs, Asians, Jews, Muslims, and any nonwhites and non-Christians. Whites belong in America—nonwhites, however, especially Asian Americans, are understood as guests or sojourners who are merely passing through. In addition, Asian American women are further discriminated, as a white male God doubly marginalizes them based on race and gender.

Asian Americans were exploited from their first major arrival as indentured workers and sex workers. Euro-Americans only allowed Asian Americans to exist in the margins because of discrimination and fear. As a result, Asian Americans are made less worthy of God and less worthy in society. Asian Americans are understood as perpetual foreigners, creating a sense of nonbelongingness to which we attribute generations of internalized misunderstandings.

Eurocentric Christianity caused enslavement, death, suffering, and *han*. Christianity in the United States furthers these acts of violence by practicing and enabling racism, discrimination, xenophobia, and sexism toward Asian American women.

God and country have become united, where being a good Christian means being a good "American," which excludes Asian Americans. Therefore, there is suspicion against Asian Americans, as exemplified during World War II when Japanese Americans were rounded up and placed in internment camps. Since Asian Americans are understood as foreigners, we are easily blamed when something goes wrong, such as when the economy goes down, when unemployment is up, or when a pandemic, such as COVID-19, happens.

This nationalistic breed of Christianity reflects the conquering spirit of those who invaded this land, constructing an understanding of salvation suffused with ideas of white supremacy. Salvation is limited to those whom the social structures are designed to privilege. Those made to be inferior, such as Asian Americans, are told that they can gain salvation if they embrace assimilation with colonized minds. White Christianity only seeks to help and save itself. To liberate Jesus from this theology means that we must dissociate Jesus from hate and fear toward people of color.[4] Asian Americans must decolonize a white Jesus and a white Christianity. The beautiful salvific elements within Asian American culture, religion, and history must be redeemed to save us from a destructive white Christianity. A redemptive salvation for all people needs to be reimagined, explored, and reinstated as the essence of Christianity.

Theology of Visibility

Jesus is the representation of divinity in human form. He is the declaration of our divine humanity, showing what it means to be connected to others, to love our neighbors and our enemies, to care for the marginalized, and to love God. When we think about Asian Americans as marginalized people, we recognize power imbalance and the need to give them their agency. Jesus shows us how to do this not by lording his authority over others but by graciously serving them, by hearing the word of God and living it out (Luke 8:19–21).

Jesus wants reconciliation through worship and by losing one's life to find life. It is in relating to others—the poor, the sick, and the outcasts—that Jesus reveals himself as the liberator, reconciler, and healer, all through a fallible human form.[5] It is in relating to the marginalized that we, like Jesus, reveal ourselves to be liberators and healers of our own spirits, our own minds. That is why Asian Americans must ally with one another—one marginalized being to another, one woman to another—and inhabit new centers of visibility that radically uplift our being. Together, in forging a new space to be seen, we can find God's teachings and reflect them back into our actions, our lives. God is present among the invisible who are seeking new ways of being in Jesus's gospel. Asian American women's experiences of invisibility, in both society and church, compel us to unpack a white patriarchal God and push us to reimagine a God who loves all people.

Jesus was born of a simple Jewish woman who raised him among other poor and marginalized people. His ministry was to proclaim the good news to the poor, "proclaim release to the captives and recovery of sight to the blind, to let the oppressed go free" (Luke 4:18). In this way, Jesus was radical in how he associated with the marginalized, the oppressed, the invisible, and the foreigners.[6] The lepers, for instance, were one of the most marginalized people of that society—shunned by the world for their misunderstood, contagious, and disfiguring disease. Yet Jesus met them, going near without fear of illness; showed them kindness; and cured them. There is much comfort in this story for Asian Americans who are often shunned by dominant white society.

The Syrophoenician woman who exhibited great faith (Matt 15:21–28), the good Samaritan who shows us how we are to be one another's neighbor (Luke 10:29–37), and the centurion who demonstrated concern for his ill servant (Luke 7:1–10)—these stories provide hope for Asian American women. Jesus is the ultimate liberator who frees the marginalized, and this gives hope to us all.

Sacred Encounter

Though Asian Americans are a largely sidelined minority, Asian American women have long been the obscured of the obscured. They are part of the invisible periphery to the wider minority landscape. Asian American women are doubly marginalized by their own Asian culture and Western culture. They have been subjected to traditional patriarchy, and for too long—like all minority women—they have had to battle undignified depictions of who they are. Alone, they have had to adapt in a cross-cultural setting, shifting expectations of sex and race in their ethnic communities and in the wider world.

Even as this happens, Jesus lifts Asian American women up and places them in an empowering space. The theological concept of invisibility is explored to understand how the marginalized and outcasts can be welcomed into the kin-dom of God. Invisibility is a spiritual issue. People of color, women, and queer and disabled persons have been made invisible throughout much of church history, and even in our modern times, the marginalized still struggle. Being part of God's kin-dom is being given agency, voice, and visibility so that all people are welcome into the church and kin-dom of God.

Understanding the richness in Asian culture, history, and religion, a theology of visibility brings to light the struggles and triumphs of Asian Americans. Through the embrace of their own culture, Asian Americans will continue to create innovative ways of thinking and speaking about God and God's presence in the world. As we bring new ways of being and understanding, we can build a new church that welcomes and embraces all people.

The church needs to embrace Asian American's gifts and leadership. Though racism must be eradicated from the church, we must not forget to include race in our theological discussion in the blind belief that the church innately practices loving its neighbors. We must remind ourselves and others to practice hospitality and welcome those who have been rendered less visible. The church is created to be a home and school for all. It is meant to house the diverse community of the world, leaving not one person or group out.

On the day of the Pentecost, the Holy Spirit inaugurated the church by proclaiming the gospel in a multiplicity of languages. In the eschatological vision of the church in Revelation 4–7, the worshipping community comes from many nations, tribes, languages, and peoples. The church in North America might see migration as an opportunity to serve God by providing hospitality to the migrant and the alien; migration offers the church an opportunity to renew itself by rediscovering the biblical vision of the church as a diverse community. This vision views cultural, linguistic, racial, and ethnic differences as gifts from God that can enrich the church's worship, deepen its sense of fellowship, and broaden its witness to God's reconciling mission in the world.[7] Thus, the Asian American immigrant church adds richness to the white church. As it does, it reminds us to embrace a theology of visibility.

A theology of visibility reminds us that everyone is a child of God, and all life is sacred. As such, we should love and embrace one another—not stereotype, racialize, discriminate against, and hate. As we live with sacredness, dignity, and love, we will recognize God who is among us and who embraces the invisible.

Acknowledgments

In the midst of completing the manuscript of this book last April, the unthinkable happened. My document—along with the entire contents of my computer—was lost irrevocably. I was writing the conclusion to chapter 4 when my keyboard suddenly stopped working, an ominous black flooded the screen, and there appeared a small white loading symbol that began to rotate and blink endearingly. I thought it was a regular software update—innocuous enough—but after trying to press every key and restarting, the loading only continued on, going for several hours until the screen finally went blank, and the fan of the computer engine halted. It was then that I realized my computer was not updating; it was crashing.

When I finally was able to turn it back on several days later, the computer was immutable. After years of researching, writing, editing, and rewriting, my project, in a matter of moments, was lost in a deadly wipe. I was inconsolable—caught in the shock and agony of lost work and, even more painful, lost time. For months, I exhausted every option trying to recover anything I could, going to every expert and every specialist—but in the end, it was unsalvageable. In my devastation and anguish, I pushed the project to the back of my mind; it was simply too painful to think about. How could I even begin to start anew? How could I return to the impossibility of the blank page?

For weeks, in between crying and panicking, I merely stared at my brand-new, empty laptop. But in the end, it was a choice of not how to begin again but when. My return to the blank page was inspired not by fate or mere obligation but by a promise—a commitment to bring a story, a people, and a history to the forefront of my reality. The task reminded me again of my responsibility to bring voice to the voiceless and color to the invisible. Thus, three months after my work was lost, I commenced the work again. The blank page that was so stifling before became a place for reinvention, and eventually, it became the place I returned to again to reshape and retell a story that is so closely a part of my own: the story of invisible Asian American women.

I truly could not have begun the process of rewriting and completing this book without the essential support of many of my friends, colleagues, and family members who lit the darkened path to completion. I am humbled by the endearing support from Susan Shaw, Rev. Jesse Jackson, Miguel De La Torre, Kwok Pui Lan, Janice Laidlaw Butler, Joseph Cheah, Nancy Bowman, Stephanie Crumley-Effinger, and Matt Hisrich, whose encouragement and unwavering advocacy gave me sustenance in the most difficult times of writing. I am forever grateful to Don McKim, Mark Koenig, Caroline Morris, and Brian Fraser for reviewing parts of the manuscript and providing crucial feedback and suggestions. I am deeply grateful to my research assistant, Bruce Marold, whose abiding critical eye and meticulous editing raised the lost book from the ashes to where it is today. I am also deeply thankful for the work of Naomi Faith Bu, who helped resculpt and strengthen this manuscript with her acutely modern perspective.

I am indebted to my editor, Emily King at Fortress Press, not only for her edits but for her essential suggestions, guidance, and patience. It was a true honor and delight to work with her before getting the book ready to print.

And to my family: my wonderful husband, who softened the tears that fell when I lost my book and began the tedious process of rewriting it; my children, Theodore, Elisabeth, and Joshua, who were there for me with warm drinks, sweet treats, and gently spoken words of encouragement when I pressed on with my second version of the manuscript; and to my sister and her family, who continued to show me love and the meaning of family through their beautiful meals and sustained nourishment. Lastly, I thank the elders: my father-in-law, who passed away in early summer 2020, who showed me that perseverance is important; my own father, who first brought me to the church and introduced me to God; and my mother, who this book was written in mind for, the woman who was and is everything to me, the woman who led a life invisible to so much of society but who was so absolute, indispensable, momentous, and vibrantly complex to those who knew her and crossed her path. I thank her for proving to me that invisibility is in the eye of the beholder, I thank her for renewing my perceptions of the world and those in it, but above all, I thank her for offering me the greatest gift I could receive: a way of seeing.

Thank you, Umma, for teaching me how to see.

Notes

Introduction

1 Jordan Liz, "State Racism, Social Justice, and the COVID-19 Pandemic," *PPJ* 3, no. 1 (2020): 4.

2 For more information, see "The Myth of the Model Minority," ISAASE, accessed July 12, 2020, https://isaase.org/myth -model-minority.

3 Ada María Isasi-Díaz introduced the word *kin-dom* to the public discourse after she heard her friend Georgen Wilson, a Franciscan nun, use it. Isasi-Díaz believed this term helped describe the liberation of God at work among people. Liberation is found in this world and not just in the life after death. Melissa Florer-Bixler, "The Kin-dom of Christ," *Sojourners*, November 20, 2018, https://sojo.net/ articles/kin-dom-christ.

Chapter 1

1 This story is drawn from Grace Ji-Sun Kim, "On Being an Asian American Woman Theologian," Faith & Leadership, April 14, 2020, https:// faithandleadership.com/grace-ji-sun -kim-being-asian-american-woman -theologian.

2 Grace Ji-Sun Kim, *The Grace of Sophia: A Korean North American Women's Christology* (Cleveland: Pilgrim, 2002), 43. Subsequent page numbers from this source will appear parenthetically in the text.

3 Cho Kyung Won, "Overcoming Confucian Barriers: Changing

Educational Opportunities for Women in Korea," in *Women of Japan and Korea: Continuity and Change*, ed. Joyce Gelb and Marian Lief Palley (Philadelphia: Temple University Press, 1944), 209.

4   Soon Man Rhim, "The Status of Women in Traditional Korean Society," in *Korean Women in a Struggle for Humanization*, ed. Harold Hakwon Sunoo and Dong Soo Kim (Princeton, NJ: Association of Korean Christian Scholars in North America, 1978), 12.

5   Denise Carmody, *Women and World Religions*, 2nd ed. (London: Pearson, 1988), 97.

6   Nantawan Boonprasat Lewis, "An Overview of the Role of Women in Asia—a Perspective and Challenge to Higher Education," *East Asia Journal of Theology* 3 (1985): 141.

7   Julia Ching, *Chinese Religions* (Maryknoll, NY: Orbis, 1993), 167.

8   Sung Hee Lee, "Women's Liberation Theology as the Foundation for Asian Theology," *East Asia Journal of Theology* 4 (1986): 5.

9   Yung-Chung Kim, *Women of Korea: A History from Ancient Times to 1945* (Seoul: Ewha Womans University Press, 1977), 84, 86.

10 Won, "Overcoming Confucian Barriers," 209.

11 Inn Sook Lee, "Korean American Women and Ethnic Identity," in *Korean American Ministry: A Resource Book*, ed. Sang Hyun Lee and John V. Moore (Louisville: General Assembly Council, 1993), 194.

12 Maxine Hong Kingston, *The Woman Warrior: Memoirs of a Girlhood among Ghosts* (New York: Vintage, 1989).

13 Gary Y. Okihiro, *Margins and Mainstreams: Asian in American History and Culture* (Seattle: University of Washington Press, 1994), 64, 65.

14 Okihiro, 64, 65.

15 Ji-soo Kim, "Kim Bok-Dong Still Fighting for Sex Slave Victims," *Korea Times*, August 17, 2016, http://www .koreatimes.co.kr/www/news/people/ 2016/08/178_212108.html.

16 "Life as a 'Comfort Woman': Story of Kim Bok-Dong | STAY CURIOUS #9," Asian Boss, YouTube, October 27, 2018, https://www.youtube.com/watch?v= qsT97ax_Xb0.

17 Erin Blakemore, "The Brutal History of Japan's 'Comfort Women,'" History.com, February 20, 2018, https://www.history .com/news/comfort-women-japan -military-brothels-korea.

18 Kazuko Watanabe, "Trafficking in Women's Bodies, Then and Now: The Issue of Military 'Comfort Women,'" *Women's Studies Quarterly* 27, nos. 1/2 (1999): 21, http://www.jstor.org/stable/ 40003395.

19 "Life as a 'Comfort Woman.'"

20 Watanabe, "Trafficking in Women's Bodies," 27.

21 "Life as a 'Comfort Woman.'"

22 Watanabe, "Trafficking in Women's Bodies," 20.

23 Norimitsu Onishi, "Denial Reopens Wounds of Japan's Ex–Sex Slaves," *New York Times*, March 23, 2007.

24 Alex Yorichi, *Japanese Prisoner of War Interrogation Report No. 49*, United States Office of War Information Psychological Warfare Team attached to U.S. Army Forces India-Burma Theater, APO 689, October 1, 1944, https://en.wikisource .org/wiki/Japanese_Prisoner_of_War _Interrogation_Report_49.

25 Sarah Chunghee Soh, *The Comfort Women: Sexual Violence and Postcolonial Memory in Korea and Japan* (Chicago: University of Chicago Press, 2009).

26 Barry S. Levy and Victor W. Sidel, eds., *War and Public Health*, 2nd ed. (Oxford: Oxford University Press, 2007), 190.

27 George Hicks, "The 'Comfort Women,'" in *The Japanese Wartime Empire*, ed. Peter Duus, Ramon Hawley Myers, and Mark R. Peattie (Princeton, NJ: Princeton University Press, 1996), 320.

28 "Life as a 'Comfort Woman.'"

29 Onishi, "Denial Reopens Wounds."

Chapter 2

1 Tamara C. Ho, "The Complex Heterogeneity of Asian American Identity," in *T&T Clark Handbook of Asian American Biblical Hermeneutics*, ed. Seung Ai Yang and Uriah Kim (New York: Bloomsbury / T&T Clark, 2019), 17.

2 Erika Lee, *The Making of Asian America: A History* (New York: Simon & Schuster, 2015), 3, 4.

3 Karen Mahajan, "The Two Asia Americas," *New Yorker*, October 21, 2015, https://www.newyorker.com/books/page-turner/the-two-asian-americas.

4 Lee, *Making of Asian America*, 4.

5 Lee, 5.

6 Cathy Park Hong, *Minor Feelings: An Asian American Reckoning* (New York: One World, 2020), 19.

7 Ronald Takaki, *A History of Asian Americans: Strangers from a Different Shore* (Boston: Little, Brown, 1989), 31–36.

8 "The Burlingame-Seward Treaty, 1868," Office of the Historian, accessed May 10, 2020, https://history.state.gov/milestones/1866-1898/burlingame-seward-treaty.

9 Hong, *Minor Feelings*, 20.

10 Joseph Cheah and Grace Ji-Sun Kim, *Theological Reflections on "Gangnam Style": A Racial, Sexual and Cultural Critique* (New York: Palgrave Macmillan, 2014), 12.

11 Cheah and Kim, 10.

12 "Naturalization Act of 1790," Densho Encyclopedia, accessed June 4, 2020, http://encyclopedia.densho.org/Naturalization_Act_of_1790/.

13 Sunny Woan, "White Sexual Imperialism: A Theory of Asian Feminist Jurisprudence," *Washington and Lee Journal of Civil Rights and Social Justice* 4, no. 2 (2008): 278.

14 Hong, *Minor Feelings*, 20.

15 Okihiro, *Margins and Mainstreams*, 77.

16 Kerry Abrams, "Polygamy, Prostitution, and the Federalization of Immigration Law," *Columbia Law Review* 105, no. 3 (April 2005): 641, 662.

17 Takaki, *History of Asian Americans*, 121.

18 Cheah and Kim, *Theological Reflections*, 13.

19 Hong, *Minor Feelings*, 21–22.

20 Hong, 21.

21 Fred Barbash, "Birthright Citizenship: A Trump-Inspired History Lesson on the 14th Amendment," *Washington Post*, October 30, 2018, https://tinyurl.com/zfpm3wsn.

22 Grace Ji-Sun Kim, "Trump's Disastrous Week of Presidency: The Chinese Exclusion Act and the Muslim Ban," HuffPost, January 30, 2017, https://tinyurl.com/v3bemkh8.

23 William Wei, "The Chinese-American Experience: An Introduction," Chinese American Experience: 1857–1892, HarpWeek, accessed November 13, 2014, https://immigrants.harpweek.com/ChineseAmericans/1Introduction/BillWeiIntro.htm.

24 Hong, *Minor Feelings*, 22.

25 Lee, *Making of Asian America*, 8.

26 Eleazar S. Fernandez, "American from the Hearts of a Diasporized People," in *Realizing the America of Our Hearts: Theological Voices of Asian Americans*, ed. Fumitaka Matsuoka and Eleazar S. Fernandez (St. Louis: Chalice, 2003), 256.

27 *Paper sons* and *paper daughters* were terms used to refer to Chinese who were born in China and immigrated illegally to the United States by buying false documentation stating that they were blood relatives to Chinese Americans who already became American citizens. A picture bride was a bride who was paired up by a matchmaker and family using pictures. This method was practiced in the early twentieth century by immigrant

male workers (mostly from Japan and Korea) who needed a bride from their native countries.

28 Ho, "Complex Heterogeneity," 17–18.

29 Sucheng Chan, *Asian Americans: An Interpretive History* (New York: Twayne, 1991), 15.

30 Kim, *Grace of Sophia*, 66.

31 Mary Paik Lee, *Quiet Odyssey: A Pioneer Korean Woman in America*, ed. and with an introduction by Sucheng Chan (Seattle: University of Washington Press, 1990), lvi, lvii.

32 Hong, *Minor Feelings*, 13.

33 Fumitaka Matsuoka, *Out of Silence: Emerging Themes in Asian American Churches* (Cleveland: Pilgrim, 1995), 73, 74; Jung Ha Kim, *Bridge-Makers and Cross-Bearers* (Atlanta: Scholars, 1997), 93, 97.

34 Kim, *Bridge-Makers*, 16.

35 One may say our cultural heritage was submerged in the Euro-American culture that dominated North America. By weight of numbers, Asian populations asserted themselves in enclaves similar to the clusters of Italians, Irish, Germans, Jews, and French in North America, making themselves a part of the community culture by creating Chinatowns, Japan Towns, Korea Towns, and even Vietnam enclaves.

36 In the late nineteenth century, Russian sociologist Jacques Novikow coined the term in the essay "Le péril jaune" ("The Yellow Peril"; 1897). The underlying racial anxieties are much older and can be traced all the way back to the Mongol invasions of Europe in the thirteenth century. In the nineteenth and twentieth centuries, the concept was established as a topos in Western adventure literature and science fiction. Prominent examples include Dr. Fu Manchu, the archetype of the Asian villain created by British author Sax Rohmer in a series of novels launched in 1913, and the emperor Ming the Merciless of the popular space-opera comic *Flash Gordon*, conceived by Alex Raymond in 1934. Cécile Heim, Boris Vejdovsky, and Benjamin Pickford, eds., *The Genres of Genre: Form, Formats, and Cultural Formations*, 1st ed. (Tubingen, Germany: Narr Francke Attempto Verlag, 2019), 108n4.

37 "Regardless of their racial and ethnic backgrounds, all immigrants resented being confined like criminals behind barbed wire fences, locked doors, and wire netted windows. 'I had never seen such a prison-like place as Angel Island,' recalled Kamechiyo Takahashi, a young Japanese bride in 1917. Many questioned as she did, 'Why I had to be kept in a prison?'" Erika Lee and Judy Yung, *Angel Island: Immigrant Gateway to America* (Oxford: Oxford University Press, 2010), loc. 1362–64, Kindle.

38 Paul Spickard, *Almost All Aliens: Immigration, Race, and Colonialism in American History and Identity* (London: Routledge, 2007), 421, 422.

39 Ellie Kanda and Mansi Gokani, "The 1871 Chinese Massacre—the Worst Lynching in U.S. History," *Peter Paccone* (blog), June 26, 2019, https://ppaccone.medium.com/the-1871-chinese-massacre-e40d601a6376.

40 Hong, *Minor Feelings*, 21–22.

41 Kelly Wallace, "Forgotten Los Angeles History: The Chinese Massacre of 1871," Los Angeles Public Library, May 19, 2017, https://www.lapl.org/collections-resources/blogs/lapl/chinese-massacre-1871.

42 "Japanese Internment Camps," History.com, October 20, 2009, https://www.history.com/topics/world-war-ii/japanese-american-relocation.

43 Christine Sismondo, "What Canada's 'Yellow Peril' Teaches Us about This Migrant Moment," *Macleans*, March 19, 2017, https://www.macleans.ca/news/canada/what-canadas-yellow-peril-teaches-us-about-this-migrant-moment/.

44 Sismondo.

45 Wing Chung Ng, *The Chinese in Vancouver, 1945–80: The Pursuit of Identity and Power* (Vancouver: University of British Columbia Press, 1999), 120–21.

46 Everett V. Stonequist, *The Marginal Man: A Study in Personality and Cultural Conflict* (New York: Russell & Russell, 1961), 149.

47 Jung Young Lee, *Marginality: The Key to Multicultural Theology* (Minneapolis: Fortress, 1995), 46.

48 Lee.

49 Peter C. Phan, *Christianity with an Asian Face: Asian American Theology in the Making* (Maryknoll, NY: Orbis, 2003), 9.

50 Peter C. Phan, "The Dragon and the Eagle: Toward a Vietnamese American Theology," in Matsuoka and Fernandez, *Realizing the America*, 165.

51 Sang Hyun Lee, "Marginality as Coerced Liminality: Toward an Understanding of the Context of Asian American Theology," in Matsuoka and Fernandez, *Realizing the America*, 13.

52 Phan, "Dragon and the Eagle," 165.

53 Victor Turner, *The Ritual Process: Structure and Anti-structure* (New York: Walter de Gruyter, 1995), 95.

54 Helene Cixous, "Castration or Decapitation?," *Signs* 7, no. 1 (Autumn 1981): 51.

55 Nami Kim, "Collaborative Dissonance: Gender and Theology in Asian Pacific America," *Journal of Race, Ethnicity, and Religion* 3 (2012): 1.

Chapter 3

1 The term *Oriental* was found offensive by natives of the Far East, since the word was originally applied to what we commonly refer to as the Levant and Egypt. There are numerous Oriental research institutes that use the term correctly, since their area of study is Anatolia, Syria, Iraq, Iran, Arabia, and Egypt. For example, see the Oriental Institute at the University of Chicago (https://oi.uchicago.edu/).

2 Rakesh Kochhar and Anthony Cilluffo, "Income Inequality in the U.S. Is Rising Most Rapidly among Asians," Pew Research Center, July 12, 2018, https://tinyurl.com/3fpcn9ck.

3 Presently, this is done by the US Customs and Border Protection agency, which is the largest armed force in the government outside of the military. By using this force, the government can employ military tactics without breaking the constitutional prohibition against using the military for internal law enforcement. (State militias are exempt from that rule, as they are controlled by the governor of each state.)

4 Erika Lee, *America for Americans: A History of Xenophobia in the United States* (New York: Basic Books, 2019), 7, 8.

5 "Immigration Act of 1917 (Barred Zone Act)," Immigration History, accessed October 5, 2020, https://immigrationhistory.org/item/1917-barred-zone-act/.

6 Lee, *America for Americans*, 11.

7 "Nationality Act of 1790," Immigration History, accessed October 5, 2020, https://immigrationhistory.org/item/1790-nationality-act/.

8 Lee, *America for Americans*, 5.

9 Dina Gerdeman, "Minorities Who 'Whiten' Job Resumes Get More Interviews," Harvard Business School, May 17, 2017, https://hbswk.hbs.edu/item/minorities-who-whiten-job-resumes-get-more-interviews.

10 Lee, *America for Americans*, 11.

11 Lee, 12.

12 Michael Keevak, "The Chinese Were White—until White Men Called Them Yellow," This Week in Asia, February 3, 2019, https://tinyurl.com/ep7bt79f.

13 Stanley Barrett, *Is God a Racist? The Right Wing in Canada* (Toronto: University of Toronto Press, 1987), 308, 309.

14 Fumitaka Matsuoka, *The Color of Faith: Building Community in a Multiracial Society* (Cleveland: United Church Press, 1998), 3.

15 Grace Ji-Sun Kim, "Asian American Feminist Theology," in *Liberation Theologies in the United States: An Introduction*, ed. Anthony Pinn and Stacey M. Floyd-Thomas (New York: New York University Press, 2010), 143.

16 Andrew Young Choi, Tania Israel, and Hotaka Maeda, "Development and Evaluation of the Internalized Racism in Asian Americans Scale (IRAAS)," *Journal of Counseling Psychology* 64 (2017): 60–64.

17 Lee, *Making of Asian America*, 374.

18 Yuan She, "Globalization and 'Asian Values': Teaching and Theorizing Asian American Literature," *College Literature* 32, no. 1 (2005): 88.

19 Lee, *Making of Asian America*, 9.

20 Michael Luo, "An Open Letter to the Woman Who Told My Family to Go Back to China," *New York Times*, October 9, 2016.

21 Anna Russell, "The Rise of Coronavirus Hate Crimes," *New Yorker*, March 17, 2020, https://www.newyorker.com/news/letter-from-the-uk/the-rise-of-coronavirus-hate-crimes.

22 Alex Ellerbeck, "Over 30 Percent of Americans Have Witnessed COVID-19 Bias against Asians, Poll Says," NBC, April 28, 2020, https://tinyurl.com/3u2snjxm.

23 Lee, *Making of Asian America*, 373.

24 Agnes Constante, "Largest U.S. Refugee Group Struggling with Poverty 45 Years after Resettlement," NBC News, March 4, 2020, https://tinyurl.com/cfb52kvp.

25 Lee, *Making of Asian America*, 373–74.

26 Lee, *Marginality*, 34.

27 Lee, 35.

28 Lee, 47.

29 Lee, 56.

30 Lee, 58.

31 Lee, 60.

32 Lee, 31.

33 Lee, 32.

34 Lee, *America for Americans*, 8.

35 Homi K. Bhabha, "The Other Question: Difference, Discrimination and the Discourse of Colonialism," in *Out There: Marginalization and Contemporary Cultures*, ed. Russell Ferguson et al. (New York: New Museum of Contemporary Art, 1990), 71, 72.

36 Grace Ji-Sun Kim, *The Holy Spirit, Chi, and the Other: A Model of Global and Intercultural Pneumatology* (New York: Palgrave Macmillan, 2011), 77.

37 Kim, 73.

38 bell hooks, "Marginality as Site of Resistance," in Ferguson et al., *Out There*, 343.

39 hooks, 343.

40 hooks, 342.

41 Kay J. Anderson, *Vancouver's Chinatown: Racial Discourse in Canada, 1875–1980* (Montreal: McGill-Queen's University Press, 1999), 18.

42 Vitor Westhelle, "Multiculturalism, Postcolonialism, and the Apocalyptic," in *Theology and the Religions: A Dialogue*, ed. Viggo Mortensen (Grand Rapids: Wm. B. Eerdmans, 2003), 10.

43 Shelly Grabe and Janey Hyde, "Ethnicity and Body Dissatisfaction among Women in the United States: A Meta-analysis," *Psychological Bulletin* 132, no. 4 (2006): 625.

44 "Whitewashing in Film," Wikipedia, last updated April 28, 2021, https://en.wikipedia.org/wiki/Whitewashing_in_film.

45 Cheah and Kim, *Theological Reflections*, 10.

46 For more discussion on understanding "Gangnam Style," see Cheah and Kim.

47 Setsu Shigematsu and Keith L. Camacho, "Introduction: Militarized Currents, Decolonizing Futures," in *Militarized*

Currents: Toward a Decolonized Future in Asia and the Pacific (Minneapolis: University of Minnesota Press, 2010), xxv–xxvi.

48 "Korean Military Brides," Asian American Activism: The Continuing Struggle, accessed June 16, 2020, https://tinyurl .com/shrkf6u9.

49 Hua Hsu, "The Stories We Tell, and Don't Tell, about Asian-American Lives," *New Yorker*, July 17, 2019, https://tinyurl .com/59u8df9n.

Chapter 4

1 A version of this reflection appears in my foreword to Grace Joseph Hill's book *Salt, Light, and a City: Conformation-Ecclesiology for the Global Missional Community* (Eugene: Cascade, 2019), 2, 3.

2 Elisabeth Schussler Fiorenza, *But She Said: Feminist Practices of Biblical Interpretation* (Boston: Beacon, 1992), 105.

3 Fiorenza, 105.

4 Fiorenza, 203.

5 Philip Connor, "6 Facts about South Korea's Growing Christian Population," FactTank: News in the Numbers, Pew Research Center, August 12, 2014, https://www.pewresearch.org/fact-tank/ 2014/08/12/6-facts-about-christianity -in-south-korea/; Jeffrey M. Jones, "U.S. Church Membership down Sharply in Past Two Decades," Gallup, April 18, 2019, https://news.gallup.com/poll/ 248837/church-membership-down -sharply-past-two-decades.aspx.

6 Harry H. L. Kitano and Roger Daniels, *Asian Americans: Emerging Minorities* (Upper Saddle River, NJ: Prentice Hall, 1988), 122.

7 Ai Ra Kim, *Women's Struggle for a New Life* (Albany: State University of New York Press, 1996), 67.

8 Eui-Young Yu and Earl H. Phillips, *Korean Women in Transition: At Home and Abroad* (Los Angeles: Center for Korean-American and Korean Studies, California State University, 1987), 289, 290.

9 Kim, *Women's Struggle*, 52.

10 Kim, *Bridge-Makers*, 135.

11 Kim, *Women's Struggle*, 368.

12 For more discussion on Korea American identity, see Lee, *Marginality*.

13 For more discussion on Wisdom Christology, see Kim, *Grace of Sophia*.

14 For more discussion on the Spirit God, see Grace Ji-Sun Kim, *Embracing the Other: The Transformative Spirit of Love* (Grand Rapids: Wm. B. Eerdmans, 2015).

Chapter 5

1 I have reflected more expansively on this in Grace Ji-Sun Kim, *The Holy Spirit: Hand-Raisers, Han and the Holy Ghost* (Minneapolis: Fortress, 2018).

2 *Jeong* is a Korean term that means "affection," "love," "empathy," and "compassion." It is a broad term that encompasses endearing emotions that permeate the Korean way of living and being. *Jeong* is often described as "sticky love," which you can experience by dipping your fingers into a jar of honey. The stickiness of the honey pulls the fingers together and makes it difficult to separate them. Similarly, *jeong* brings people together through a sticky love that binds friends, family, and communities together.

3 "Trinh T. Minh-ha," Center for Cultural Studies, University of California Santa Cruz, accessed June 25, 2020, https:// culturalstudies.ucsc.edu/inscriptions/ volume-34/trinh-t-minh-ha/.

4 Trinh T. Minh-ha, "Cotton and Iron," in Ferguson et al., *Out There*, 328.

5 Minh-ha, 330, 331.

6 hooks, "Marginality as Site," 341.

7 hooks, 332.

8 hooks, 342.

9 hooks, 104.

10 hooks, 342.

11 hooks, 343.

12 Steed Vernyl Davidson, *Empire and Exile: Postcolonial Readings of the Book of Jeremiah* (New York: T&T Clark International, 2011), 103.

13 Grace Ji-Sun Kim and Susan Shaw, *Intersectional Theology: An Introductory Guide* (Minneapolis: Fortress, 2018), 2.

14 Fiorenza, *But She Said*, 202.

15 Vivian M. May, *Pursuing Intersectionality, Unsettling Dominant Imaginaries* (New York: Routledge, 2015), 3.

16 Alison Bailey explains, "Race and gender should be conceptualized not as 'race + gender,' instead they should be thought of in terms of 'gendered racism' or how 'gender is racialized.' It makes sense [from an intersectional approach] to talk about capitalist patriarchies rather than capitalism and patriarchy" (quoted in May, 3–4).

17 Kim and Shaw, *Intersectional Theology*, 9.

18 Kim and Shaw, xiv.

19 Kim and Shaw.

20 Cheah and Kim, *Theological Reflections*, 88.

21 "What Is the Concept of 'Already but Not Yet'?," Got Questions, accessed October 24, 2020, https://www.gotquestions.org/already-not-yet.html.

22 Cheah and Kim, *Theological Reflections*, 88, 89.

23 Cheah and Kim, 89.

24 Cheah and Kim, 89.

25 Cheah and Kim, 89.

26 Grace Ji-Sun Kim, "They'll Know We Are Christians by Our 'Jeong': Five Asian Concepts That Can Deepen Our Understanding of the Holy Spirit," *Sojourners*, February 2019, https://sojo.net/magazine/february-2019/they-ll-know-we-are-christians-our-jeong.

27 This is a central theme in Willie James Jennings, *Acts* (Louisville: Westminster John Knox, 2017), his boundary-breaking commentary on Luke's account of the formation of the early church.

28 Kim, "They'll Know."

29 *Panentheistic* means "all in God," or the understanding that the universe is a manifestation of God.

30 Joe Hellerman, "Is Group-First Christianity a Trans-cultural Value?," *Good Book Blog*, May 4, 2017, https://www.biola.edu/blogs/good-book-blog/2017/is-group-first-christianity-a-trans-cultural-value.

31 Kim, "They'll Know."

32 Kim.

33 Kim.

34 Plotinus studied Plato and believed that the universe emanates from "the One," through "Intellect-Mind" (*nous* in Greek) and "Soul" (*psyche*). Each of these three is called a hypostasis. By Augustine, *hypostasis* became a term for "persons" of the Trinity. Augustine's conception of the Holy Spirit is based on Plotinus's third hypostasis and his understanding of reason (Logos). This means that he understood it as soul and reason. Thomas L. Humphries Jr., "Augustine and the Holy Spirit," review of *The Spirit of Augustine's Early Theology*, by Chad Tyler Gerber, *Marginalia*, July 8, 2014, https://marginalia.lareviewofbooks.org/augustine-holy-spirit/.
Augustine's theology has influenced how Christians view the Holy Spirit as an abstract concept rather than an embodied being.

35 Kim, "They'll Know."

36 Kim.

37 Kim.

38 Women were biblically viewed as "helpers" and thus have been cast as subordinate to men. Augustine viewed women in this way, and his influence has been felt for much of Christian history.

For further discussion, see Elizabeth
A. Clark, *Women in the Early Church:
Message of the Fathers of the Church*

(Wilmington, DE: Michael Glazier,
1983), 13:40.

Conclusion

1   Abby Budiman, "Key Findings about
    U.S. Immigrants," Pew Research
    Center, August 20, 2020, https://
    www.pewresearch.org/fact-tank/
    2020/08/20/key-findings-about-u-s
    -immigrants/.
2   Lee, *Marginality*, 33.
3   "Fides quaerens intellectum" (Faith
    seeking understanding) is Anselm's
    motto, which means "active love of God
    seeking a deeper knowledge of God." See
    Stanford Encyclopedia of Philosophy, s.v.
    "Saint Anselm," last updated December 8,
    2020, https://plato.stanford.edu/entries/
    anselm/.
4   Miguel De La Torre, *Burying White
    Privilege: Resurrecting a Badass Christianity*
    (Grand Rapids: Wm. B. Eerdmans,
    2019), 27, 28.
5   Cheah and Kim, *Theological Reflections*,
    88.
6   Cheah and Kim, 89.
7   Safwat Marzouk, *Intercultural Church*
    (Minneapolis: Fortress, 2019), 3.

Index